Veronica McCall

AGAINST ALL ODDS, PERSEVERE!

Stories of our Sisters...

Verses marked KJV are taken from the King James Version of the bible

Verses marked NIV are taken from the New International Version of the bible

All the stories referenced in this book are true, but the names have been eliminated to protect the privacy of the people mentioned.

AGAINST ALL ODDS, PERSEVERE! STORIES OF OUR SISTERS...

ISBN: 978-0998526409

DEDICATION

      I dedicate this book to my beautiful mother, Lula B. McKinney. She was a devoted mother of five children, grandmother of sixteen, and great-grandmother of fifteen. She was a woman of integrity and class who created a legacy that will live on forever! We have created some wonderful memories that will last me throughout my lifetime. Watch over us all as you rest in paradise. I will continue to strive to be the best that I can be and make you very proud of me. Until we meet again …

TABLE OF CONTENTS

<u>Introduction</u>

What will you do when life happens? Stop for a minute and really ask yourself this question. Many of us often fantasize, dream about, and have our whole lives planned out to a "T" on how we anticipate things will go and play out. Most women plan their wedding out from the beginning to the end while creating that checklist of their future Prince Charming and how great marital bliss will be before they are even dating.

I remember at an early age, I had planned to be married by a certain age, have my first child at this age, my second child at that age, how many children I was going to have total, when I would finish school, buy a house, a car, and the list goes on. Our minds take us to a place with a vivid imagination of how we plan our lives to be. What we do not factor in or contemplate is what obstacles, roadblocks, detours, setbacks, heartaches, disappointments or pain that we may encounter along this journey. These key factors can alter, hinder or stop our plans partially or completely.

As we live, LIFE happens. Life is not always easy or fair. Life is not always filled with joy and happiness, and life usually does not play out as we hoped. Life is not always picture perfect, but the life you live is your story. What you do when life happens to you, makes all the difference. "…In this world you will have trouble. But take heart! I have overcome the world." (John 16:33 NIV)

This book contains several short stories of women who have faced different obstacles and challenges throughout their walk of life. It will include how these challenging situations have affected them and/or changed their lives. We will discuss how these women dealt with and made steps to overcome these obstacles when LIFE happened to them. Life for some of these women may include situations of abuse, domestic violence, divorce, loss of a loved one, being a single parent/teenage mom, battling depression or low self-esteem etc. …

When we are going through things in life, many times we feel like no one can relate, that we are the only one who has experienced this, or that we are all alone. The truth is that there are other people who have experienced the same or similar situations as you have. Life happens to all of us, but to avoid becoming stagnant, you have to leave your past behind you, fight with all of heart and soul for your happiness and peace, trust God wholeheartedly, and move forward in the destiny that HE has preplanned just for "YOU." Jeremiah 29:11 NIV states, "For I know the plans I have for you," declares the Lord, "plans to prosper you and not to harm you, plans to give you hope and a future." Your pain is an indicator of your purpose. Position yourself accordingly so that life's trials and tribulations can become the vehicle that strengthens you, builds your character and helps you to learn and grow. Let your test become your testimony that will eventually propel you as well as help others.

This is an interactive book that will cause you to think and reflect on your own life, your own story, and those individuals around you. While reading the different stories, you may also reflect on the lives of others that are connected to you. You will be empowered, you will be encouraged and you will be inspired.

You may have had your life all mapped out on how you would have loved for it to go, but in reality, no one's life goes exactly like we plan. My plans were so off course as it related to my life, at one point I had decided to stop planning altogether. At one time I had convinced myself that there was no need to plan things out anymore because the plans never work out anyway.

Now after many experiences, good and bad, I know that God has the ultimate plan for my life. I understand the power and the significance of prayer. I also know that the Bible tells me to write down my visions and make them plain and God will honor my petitions if it lines up according to his will. Now my plans include God in them because I pray and discuss them with him. I want to be led by God when making decisions, and I understand that things are always subject to change. We must make the most of each day we live, figure out our purpose, then walk in that God-given purpose.

Even as I was writing this book, I had to persevere to complete it. The adversary threw so many bricks my way in an attempt to make me want to give up. To name some of the things that I endured, I have had financial attacks, ministry attacks, several different relationship challenges, challenges on my job, computer issues, I lost information needed for the book, a strong wind storm blew a tree down on my house, and my husband broke his ankle and had to have surgery. Through all of this, I still persevered!

There were days I questioned and doubted my ability to complete this book, but I persevered! When I missed deadlines and things didn't happen as fast as I thought they would, I persevered! When things didn't seem to line up according to the plans, I persevered! On days that I didn't have it in me, I persevered! The harder I experienced struggle, the harder I persevered. It was also confirmation that because of this struggle, this book was predestined by God. I knew that many women needed to be blessed by reading this book but the enemy was trying to stop that plan. Well because I persevered, you are reading this book today.

After you read this book, my desire is that your mind and spirit are renewed and revived, that you seek God for direction for his perfect plan for your life, and that you never give up on YOU! When life happens to you, learn how to make adjustments, shake it off and continue to move onward and forward in what you are supposed to do. If you fall down, get back up again. If you fail, learn everything you can from your failures. If life throws you a curve ball, catch it, refocus, regroup and make steps to overcome it.

Never lose hope! Your destiny is calling your name. Other people are depending on you to succeed. Your purpose is waiting on you. What will you do when life happens to you, your family, your children, your friends, and others that are connected to you, you ask? Against ALL Odds, Persevere! Read what these women did, when life happened to them.

Chapter 1
Persevering

What does persevering mean to you? The word PERSEVERE is a verb, which means it requires some sort of action. The meaning of this word is to continue in a course of action even in the face of difficulty or with little or no prospect of success. When I think of someone persevering, I imagine different stages an individual may be in to overcome an obstacle.

Your stage of persevering can be determined by where you perceive your struggle to be. The first step is recognizing the depth of your struggle. How long have you been dealing with the same or similar struggles in your life? The second step is recognizing how deep, how difficult, how real your struggle is. The timeframe it takes you to overcome a particular struggle can affect your ability to successfully persevere.

"Therefore since we are surrounded by such a great cloud of witnesses, let us throw off everything that hinders and the sin that so easily entangles. And let us run with perseverance the race marked out for us, fixing our eyes on Jesus, the pioneer and perfecter of faith. For the joy set before him he endured the cross, scorning its shame, and sat down at the right hand of the throne of God. Consider him who endured such opposition from sinners, so that you will not grow weary and lose heart." (Hebrews 12:1-3 NIV)

Think about the following questions as it relates to your life. Please complete the following questions. Determine what stage of persevering you may fall into as it relates to your story and struggles.

Stages of Persevering:

Stage 1: Someone who has the desire to face their struggle
Stage 2: Someone who is thinking about ways to overcome their struggle
Stage 3: Someone who has designed a plan to overcome their struggle
Stage 4: Someone who is actively taking steps to overcome their struggle
Stage 5: Someone who has overcome their struggle
Stage 6: Someone who has overcome their struggle, who is healed from, and empowered by the struggle, and is able to help others overcome their struggle

Facing my struggles, accepting my truth:

What are some struggles that you have faced?

How difficult are or were they for you to face and why?

Rate your struggle(s) according to difficulty from 1-3.
(low, medium, high)

How long has it taken you to overcome your struggle and turn your life around?

What are your strengths and weaknesses?

What stage of persevering are you in?

What are ways in which you think a person can persevere through their struggle?

Chapter 2
Goodbye Past, Hello Future

"Always remember to fall asleep with a dream and wake up with a purpose."

My name is Ms. I Am Made New and this is my story. I am the only child and my mother and father were never married. My mother married my stepfather before I was born. On the night of their wedding, he left out of the house and didn't come back for two days. As my mother looked out of the window, she saw him get into a car with two other ladies. My mother previously lived with her aunt and uncle and she felt like she was a burden to them, so she got married and moved out to a new place. In her mind, she believed that if she didn't stay with my stepfather, she would not be able to maintain her own household alone and she would be forced to go back to living with her family. This fear crippled her into staying in an unhealthy relationship that caused her to endure great heartache and pain. Her wedding night was the first of many days and nights of infidelity, drug abuse, and unhappiness.

My mother eventually ended up having an affair with another man outside of her marriage. That person was my father and from that affair, I was conceived. But I was raised to believe that my stepfather was my biological father and the man I grew up believing was just a friend of the family was actually my real father. It was not until I was a little older that I was told the truth about who my father really was. I was about twelve years old when my mother told me this unspoken truth. I can say I was actually somewhat relieved when I was informed that my stepfather was not my biological father because of the type of person he was and how he treated my mother. My stepfather treated me very well just like I was his own daughter, but when it came to my mother, it was a different story. I still have a good relationship with him to this day. My mother and stepfather eventually ended up getting a divorce, and my parents continued to have an off and on relationship with each other. My father had his own apartment in the same complex that we lived in, but he would stay with us until he and my mother would get on each other's last nerve. When they got into a big argument, he would march back to his own place until things cooled down. Before too long, he would be back partially residing with us.

Both of my parents always worked two jobs to make ends meet. Even though they were not home most of the time, they were very strict on me and did not play when it came to foolishness. Sometimes I attended church with my parents, but most of the time I attended church with my aunt. I always viewed my mother as being private, shy, funny and a very hard-working woman. I was not able to spend much time with my parents, especially my mother because she was always gone or tired. I spent more time with my dad but deep within desired more intimate mother/daughter time with her. I wanted my mother to be more involved in my life and the activities that I was involved in. I needed her as a little girl developing into a young lady and into womanhood. As bad as

I longed for her presence, she just wasn't there for me. I became use to not having her around very much.

My father suffered from depression and paranoid schizophrenia. He was frequently in and out of the mental health institution for treatment for his illness. When my father lost his mother, that is when life really started to happen for me. This situation was so difficult for him that it caused him to go into a deep depression and he ended up having a mental breakdown. After his breakdown, my life changed forever and I literally spiraled out of control. I became fearful of him for a while because he was literally a different person. I saw him do different things that were out of the norm for his character. I remember the police pulling him over one time and he jumped out of the car and started running and the police had to chase him down. He was pepper-sprayed by the police many times, beat up, and even shot with the bean bags. I remember being so afraid that he was going to get seriously hurt or killed by the police because of his erratic behavior.

Most of his behavior left so many questions in my mind because mental illness can be hard for people to understand, especially a child. It was very difficult for me to see my father sick like this and declining right before my little brown eyes. My way of dealing with everything that was going on around me was being resentful and rebellious against both of my parents. I rejected everything my father had told me or taught me. Sometimes I went to school and other times I didn't. I began hanging out with my friends more and caring less about my own life. I was angry because I just didn't understand what was going on and why. Why was my father this way now? Why is he so out of control? I loved my father deeply but our relationship was never ever the same.

My father ended up passing away and I became even more devastated and lost. Even though in the past I didn't want to listen to him, I needed my father to teach me about men and relationships and help me with things. I had never imagined living my life without him. He was gone too soon! My emotions were in a big ball being bounced all over the place. One minute I felt free because I didn't have to worry about my father disciplining me for my out-of-control behavior and the next minute I felt lost and I didn't know how to go on without him. One minute I was relieved that I didn't have to worry about him getting hurt because of his erratic behavior and the next minute I was missing him like crazy. I didn't know how to channel or express myself and all of these emotions that I was feeling. I was really a mess! My life was a mess too.

I became pregnant at the young age of fifteen on my very first sexual encounter with my boyfriend. I gave in to peer pressure and tried this sex thing to fit in. I was scared and confused. I didn't want to tell my mother so I hid my pregnancy from her for a little while. She eventually found out that I was pregnant because one of my friends ended up spilling the beans. My mother made me take a pregnancy test to confirm it. It was indeed true — I was pregnant. I contemplated getting an abortion, but I eventually decided against that and continued with the pregnancy. I remained in my relationship with my boyfriend, but it was unhealthy and inconsistent like most areas of my life. He was abusive and he would frequently rape me. I did not want to continue to have sex with him. My life changed significantly after becoming a teenage mother. My on-again-off-again boyfriend was not consistent with helping me take care of our baby. This baby was now my responsibility. I could no longer do all the things my friends were able to do. I could not go many places anymore. I was forced to grow up really quick.

My mother became very instrumental in helping me care for my baby initially. She always tried to tell me things to try to prevent me from making the wrong decisions or prevent me from venturing down the wrong path of life. The maternal instinct in her naturally wanted to protect me from the evil of this world and keep me from a life of self-destruction. She had to continue to teach and raise me in addition to showing me how to be a mother to a newborn. I appreciated my mother and all she did for me growing up to take care of me and now my baby while guiding me along this difficult journey. I believe it was important, however, for me to experience life and certain things for myself. Life can mold you into the mature being that you must become. I had made some bad choices in my life and I had to own it and start dealing with it.

Back in the day at the church that I attended, if a young lady became pregnant you had to go in front of the entire church to confess it and apologize for your actions. I was already embarrassed and ashamed about being pregnant in the first place but knowing that I had to do this made the entire situation worse. I refused to go before the church to confess this sin, so I left the church completely. I eventually ended up dropping out of high school. I went back for a short period of time and then ended up dropping out again. I actually started working at age 13 but once I had a child of my own, I felt like I really needed to help my mother more now. So school was not an option for me at that time. I began working a full-time job with many adult responsibilities. Then my mother and I began to clash. We were always arguing and it was difficult for us to be in agreement or muddle through anymore.

One day out of the blue she decided she no longer wanted to deal with me and my bad attitude anymore. She packed up all of her things and moved out of the house with no real warning. I came home and she was gone. She told me that since I wanted to be and act like I was grown so bad, she was going to show me what it was really like to be grown and she left me to care for everything on my own. I was probably about 18 or 19 at that time. I was still very young, too young to be taking on all of this responsibility. I worked a lot of hours and made some decent money for my age, but I was irresponsible with my money. I was forced to take care of my child and myself. It was a true struggle. I could not understand why my mother would do that to me. That hurt me to my core. I eventually ended up moving into another place that was more affordable. My mother moving out and leaving abruptly forced me to be more independent, more responsible in certain areas, and more mature. I had to learn how to survive on my own, which in reality I had already done for years since my parents were in my life but really absent — but now it was more real. I had to figure out how to take care of my own and my child's needs. I refused to ask for help because I had programmed myself to believe that if I received help from someone then I was a failure. So I worked hard and pressed on to get things done.

For the majority of my life, I was in darkness. I had to work hard to discover who I really was. I lacked knowledge of what real love was. I remained in unhealthy and abusive relationships. I often times felt trapped in something I couldn't get out of even if I wanted to. I was consumed with fear of the unknown. I felt as if I had no one to turn to or talk to. I also was embarrassed and ashamed of my life and didn't want anyone to know what I was going through. I wanted to be loved and longed for it. When I think about how my mother stayed in unhealthy relationships and tried her hardest to make them work, I think about how badly she longed to be loved too and I see myself. My mother was blinded to the concepts of love, relationships, and being nurtured early because her mother left her and her siblings with family when they were young. This forced her to grow up fast to help take care of her siblings, so she never had a real childhood or what society would call "a normal life." She always had to be strong and hold everything together for everyone. She was not able to attend school or do much of anything that kids at that age did. She bottled up a lot of her emotions and held it all in while she worked and did what she needed to do to survive. To this day she still doesn't know how to express what she is feeling very well. I see myself repeating this same cycle and I have dealt with many of these same issues.

I did try traditional counseling and Christian counseling, and it does help to have someone to talk to and discuss your experiences with to an extent. The counselors will give you good ideas and suggestions as it relates to your problems, but you still have to find out what will work for you and make efforts to solve your own problems. You still have to be willing to do the work. I often wished I had done things differently in my life. I wish that I had listened to my parents more and that I could change my past — but I know that I can't. I have learned a lot from my past experiences and mistakes, and I am learning to leave them behind and keep moving forward. I held grudges for many years and I internalized a lot. This is totally not good if you want to move forward. I cannot continue to wonder why those bad experiences in my past had to happen to me. Why not me? I am not better or different than anyone else.

Instead of harboring past hurt and pain, we have to embrace the curve balls of life that come our way and learn from them, and come to know how to deal with them. I am proud to say that I no longer live under a cloud of deep darkness. Now I am generally a happy person and I love to smile. People often wonder and sometimes ask me why I smile so much. I smile because I am blessed and I smile because I am not my past, I am made new. You should never judge a book by its cover because sometimes you never know what a person has gone through in their life that causes them to react or behave the way they do. Through everything that you go through, you have to find your own happiness. I am working on building stronger and healthier relationships/friendships. I am learning to love and trust again. My past experiences left me guarded but I have begun to tear those walls down and be more open-minded. I am walking with God and desire to grow closer and closer to him. It is important to first search yourself, then find out who you are and what your needs are as a woman. Love yourself and stand up for what you believe in no matter what. You can do anything you set your mind and heart to do as long as you have the determination to act on it and see it through to the end. I know that nothing is impossible with God. As women, we need to do a better job to help empower and encourage one another instead of tear each other down. God is love and he wants us to love one another.

I have been able to accomplish some things in my life that I never thought I would be able to do. I did eventually work hard to obtain my GED. I continue to work hard to take care of my family. I have a deeper relationship with God. I have made fasting and praying a regular part of my lifestyle. I attend church on a regular basis, and through my spiritual walk, I am learning more about God, his sovereignty and his love for me. The more I realize how much God loves me, the more I grow to love myself and the more I recognize my past is forgiven. I have been separated from some of my old friends and now I have some new positive Christian friends in my life to help support and encourage me. I am learning to trust God more in every area of my life. I understand that life has its ups and downs but there is always a lesson to learn from our life experiences. I am still working on me daily and I know this is a continuous process. I am not currently married but I am working on being a better mother and preparing myself for the role of a wife with who God is preparing just for me. I can be truthful in saying that my childhood was not ideal and not what I would have chosen for myself. I wish my childhood could have been completely different but that is not humanly possible. What I can change is my future and how I walk into it. Hello Future, you are looking really bright!

"Now if we are children, then we are heirs — heirs of God and co-heirs with Christ, if indeed we share in his suffering in order that we may also share in his glory. I consider that our present sufferings are not worth comparing with the glory that will be revealed in us.

"For the creation waits in eager expectation for the children of God to be revealed. For the creation was subjected to frustration, not by its own choice, but by the will of the one who subjected it, in hope that the creation itself will be liberated from its bondage to decay and brought into the freedom and glory of the children of God." (Romans 8:17-21 NIV)

"Your beginnings will seem humble, so prosperous will your future be." (Job 8:7 NIV)

Pearls of Wisdom:

• You cannot continue to look backward at what was. Look ahead to what is to come.

• Let your downfall be your footstool to lift you higher and propel you forward.

• Set goals for yourself and take the limits off of what you can do with God.

• Pray, fast, and meditate often; this will help you get through anything.

• Do not just accept anything for yourself; set your standards high and stand firm in it.

• Celebrate all of your achievements big or small. If you don't, who will? Treat yourself to something enjoyable.

• Always encourage yourself and then support and encourage others.

• Do not stay stuck in your past hurt and pain.

• Your past experiences are part of your testimony, not only to help you but to help others as well

I OWN IT! SESSION:

1) What challenges did Ms. I Am Made New face?

2) What would have been helpful to her during these challenges?

3) Were there any patterns or generational curses that you identified with her and her parents?

4) Is there anything in this story you can relate to?

5) What level of persevering do you believe she is in?

6) What scriptures would be helpful for her?

Chapter 3

Moving On, It Is My New Season

"Never regret a day in your life: good days give happiness, bad days give experiences, worst days give lessons, and best days give memories."

Hello, my name is Mrs. Moving Forward and this is my story. I grew up in a household where a lot of families lived in the same house with us. My family always hung out and spent time together. I have great memories of having so much fun with my family, my cousins, my aunts, and siblings. My memories included things like playing outside, playing cards and dominoes, and going out of town on vacations to Canada, Maryland, and Milwaukee and many other cities. We also went to parades, art/wax museums, Sunday school, and church. I did a lot of things growing up.

I have a very big boisterous family that has always been pretty close, supportive and they have provided a lot of guidance to me growing up. The family members that did not live with us lived in the same neighborhood close by. I viewed the men and women in my family as loving, strong, intelligent, educated and artistic. Growing up I had a variety of experiences that groomed me to be a very well-rounded individual today. I also had a relationship with God early on that created a solid foundation for my future. I believe one of the best gifts you can give a child is an enjoyable childhood creating lasting memories and a variety of well-rounded experiences. I can proudly say I did experience my childhood in this way.

At a young age, my parents got divorced and I lived with my mother. My mother took good care of me and my siblings. I do not remember much about my biological father nor the relationship I had with him prior to them divorcing or thereafter. The only memory I have of my father is when I was in the fifth grade at his funeral. Other people that knew him well have told me wonderful stories and things about my father that fills my heart with joy. I have been told that he was very intellectual, good with children and a family man. My father was well known throughout our community. He was a giving person and loved by many, especially his family. I also heard he could be controlling and a jealous person at times too. That probably contributed to my parents' divorce. I have a few pictures of my father and the memories that other people have shared with me to remember him by.

When I was only five years old, I was molested by my female babysitter who was fifteen years old and was someone that was trusted and close to my family. Both of our families were very close and spent a lot of time hanging out together. She used to talk very derogatory toward me and threatened to hurt me if I ever told anyone. She would say things to me like, "You know you like it" or "If you tell anyone, I will do this or that." I remember her being very developed because she was a lot older than I was and I remember seeing her pubic hair and that just disgusted me. The sound of her voice made me sick to my stomach. I would have to see my abuser whenever our families would socialize together. The way I dealt with this horrendous ordeal was to suppress every memory of it. I never told my mother what had happened to me and I do not discuss it much at all. To this day I occasionally run into her. My abuser is now married with children of her own. This experience did make me more cautious and protective when I had my own children. The prevalence of sexual abuse to children is difficult to truly determine because it is not often reported.

According to a U.S. Department of Health and Human Services Children's Bureau report, 9.2 percent of victimized children were sexually assaulted. About 1 in 5 girls and 1 in 20 boys is a victim of child sexual abuse. The National Institute of Justice reported 3 out of 4 adolescents who have been sexually assaulted were victimized by someone they knew well. Children who do not live with both parents have a higher risk of being sexually abused. It is so important to discuss with your children about inappropriate touching and behavior by others. Discuss scenarios with them to explain what is inappropriate or doesn't feel right and come up with solutions. Inform them not to be ashamed or feel guilty because it is not their fault. Also, have an open honest relationship with your children and explain how important it is to report an incident to you right away so that the abuse will stop and possible legal steps can be taken against the perpetrator. Have a family plan in place just in case it is needed.

While in middle and high school, I was smart, outgoing, involved in a lot of school activities and I had several friends. But I didn't tolerate drama. I was pretty popular, happy, and very secure in myself. I was confident with a strong and bold personality. I just learned to love the skin that I was in and I recognized the beauty within myself. One of my favorite songs was by Whitney Houston, "The Greatest Love of All." I use to listen to that song a lot. It reassured me at an early age to love myself, that I was great and to walk in it. As a child, I remember my family comparing the children to each other. Who was taller, thinner, prettier, who had the longest hair, who danced the best, etc. …This did at times make me feel rejected and unloved, but I did not let it affect my self-esteem. I didn't understand why all that mattered. I was always taught to love others as well, but I didn't always feel that I received that same respect and love in return. I dealt with hatred from others and I always had to defend myself. There were some individuals that would lie and hate on me for no apparent reason. My confidence oftentimes made others insecure and jealous of me. I remember when I went to the prom one year and afterward I went to the hotel with my friends. A friend of the family made up lies about me without knowing what was really going on and told my mother things that tainted my mother's eyes regarding me. The truth was that I was still a virgin and we were just a group of friends that got together to talk, play games, and enjoy our prom. It was becoming more difficult to trust anyone.

My mother got remarried and my stepfather is the only father that I have ever known. He was a fun person, but he was also mean, domineering, old-fashioned, and very strict. As I got older, I saw my mother changing a great deal. I always saw my mom as a very strong person but she appeared to me to be more passive and submissive. She didn't have much say so. Then my mother got saved, so we were always in church or Bible study and she even starting singing in the choir. I didn't see my mother as fun or cool anymore because things had changed and she was changing. I began to feel like I lost my mother and that she was no longer there for me and my siblings. Our time together had diminished. One good thing about this change is that I developed a relationship with God as a child. My mother would read Bible stories to us often and I would really look forward to that time with her. I can still visualize that big book full of beautiful pictures and amazing stories.

As a child, I learned about trusting God and having faith to believe that anything was possible. I saw the goodness and blessings of God upon my life. I had nice clothes, lived in a nice house, and I didn't experience lack. I went to school with other children that appeared to be poor, not clean, with old looking clothing, runny noses, etc. My mother and aunt always taught us that it was not right to look down on or judge others who had less than we did or lived differently. I didn't experience poverty or neglect as a child but I had a heart for others who did. My mother showed God's love by taking care of other children in the neighborhood who were not as blessed as we were. She has always been a caregiver of children when she was unsure if she would have any children of her own. To this day I have zero tolerance for people judging or looking down on others. I am a giving person that loves to help others whenever I can. I strongly believe that I have been blessed to be a blessing to others. I have a heart to give and help others whenever and however I can.

My stepfather did not show us much love or affection, so I felt rejected by him. I remember my parents arguing a lot. I lived in a very controlled and tense environment after they got married. His form of discipline was very old school and different from what we were used to. One time I remember one of my siblings being punished by being placed under water with soap in his mouth. I often felt attacked by him and my sister became depressed by it all. One time he hit me and I hit him back. I just snapped and I left the house. I was pretty much homeless. I ended up roaming around and I stayed with different family members and friends. I was under a lot of pressure, but I was one strong individual. I stopped going around my parents for a while after this. I graduated from high school and went on to college. I had my own apartment as a teenager. Due to my constantly maturing relationship with God, I was later convicted and compelled to apologize to my parents and mend our relationship. So I was obedient to

HIS will and I did just that. I apologized and made things right with my parents, even though I wasn't completely to blame. I had to learn to forgive, accept, and love my parents in spite of their faults. Due to examples of marriage and relationships growing up and my childhood experiences, as a child, I had convinced myself that I didn't believe in the idea of marriage. I had planned to have a boyfriend, but I would make my own money, have my own things, and be my own boss. If I got tired of him, I would move on. That is the attitude I had and the motto I lived by.

I became pregnant while I was in college, but I pressed on and was still able to graduate. I still wasn't fond of the idea of marriage but I was committed to having a family and a present father for my child. I experienced periods of loneliness and the strong desire and need to be loved. I wanted to give love and receive love in return. I ended up getting married to my good friend who was the father of my child. I loved him but I was not in love with him like a wife should be. I was more in love with the idea of being loved and the idea of having a family than being in love with my husband. My husband was a good father and he spent a lot of time with our children and they had a really good relationship. I lived in a really nice, big house, I was financially secure, but my marriage was unhealthy and I was not truly happy. We lived a good life, we went on many trips as a family, and our house was the party zone. Everyone loved to come over and hang out at our house.

Growing up, my husband's mother and father were together but their relationship was dysfunctional. His mother would pop in and out of their lives as she pleased and was usually drunk or high. She often left the kids, leaving my husband to take care of his siblings. His father was there physically but was usually drunk or high all the time as well. He would tend to fall or pass out from his extracurricular activities and therefore was not physically and mentally available for the children.

In the beginning of our marriage, my husband was a social drinker, but I noticed that after his father passed away his drinking increased and eventually got worse and worse. His drinking was way worse than I ever knew or even imagined it to be. My husband was an alcoholic and the worse his drinking got, the more it affected our marriage. He began drinking and partying with his friends, not only on the weekend but during the week too. Any occasion was a good cause for all of his friends to come over and hang out and drink. The drinking continued to get worse. The partying, the loud talking, laughing, and loud music continued and became more frequent. I would pray for him and with him. When I would plead for him to get help for his drinking, he would refuse. He would then tell me to get some friends to hang out with because he had friends.

Alcohol can be so detrimental to one's self and family. I believe that people think it is no big deal to drink or that it is better than drugs — but it is an addiction. When my husband drank alcohol, it made him mean and evil spirited. He would do irrational things, argue, become easily aggravated, and curse a lot. He had a bad temper and we began to argue all the time. He was always mean, always mad, and then he started to even be mean to the children. .

As time went on his mouth became more and more obnoxious and he was oblivious to reality and what was really going on in his life or with his family. At times, I would wake up in the morning to him and his friends passed out in the house. He continued to refuse counseling, and he refused to go to church too. He ended up getting laid off from his job and would not look for another job. I would have to look for job openings for him. I was use to some dysfunction, but I was not use to this type of lifestyle. I eventually realized he was not ready or willing to change and I could not continue to live in this type of environment. My husband was never physically abusive toward me, but he would have fits of rage when he was drunk. I did not want my children living in this environment and I was unsure of what they would wake up to. I was also afraid of losing it one day and not having control over what I might do to him because I could become so angry.

I began to set a plan in motion to leave my husband about three months in advance. We had been married for several years and it took me about three years before I muscled up enough strength and courage to commit to leaving. I prayed about my situation and readiness for change. I opened a separate bank account to financially prepare for the move. I assessed my finances and our safety in planning for the change. I finally ended up moving out of the house that I loved and moved closer to my immediate family. I did not tell my husband that I was leaving until the last minute. He was upset, he cried, and he asked what he could do to keep me from leaving. I knew he was not willing to put in the work and get the help he needed to make this marriage work. He was not available financially, physically, or emotionally and I felt like he had abandoned me and his family. I knew that I had to move on. This process was not an easy one to endure. It was a difficult choice to leave my husband and my lifestyle especially because I had to uproot my children. I went through a grieving process and it was a big adjustment for me and the children, but I was confident with my decision. After I left, we remained friends and he even thought about moving closer to us so that he could be closer to the children. He ended up letting his family talk him out of doing it, and this has affected his relationship with the children.

I am currently separated from my husband, taking care of my children and I plan to proceed with filing for a divorce soon. I graduated from college and I have had a successful career. One of my children has graduated from high school and is now attending college. I would one day love to be remarried to whom God has handpicked for me and to someone who I am truly in love with. I am ready to love freely, be loved and receive love. I have an even closer relationship with God now. I plan to own my own home again and I am looking forward to my bright future. I have so many creative ideas rambling around in my head that I plan to explore and bring forth. I made a decision that any way God wants to bless me, I will be satisfied. I am learning to be content with my current situation while figuring out what is important to me. I know that no matter what comes my way, I am blessed. I do not overlook the blessings of LIFE in general like breathing, walking, talking and good health. Everything we have is a blessing and we need to be thankful for it all. I am not sure how my story will end, but I am trusting God. My Advice on Love, Marriage, and Kids:

Love: Love is patient, kind, does not keep a record of wrong. You have to forgive others. Accept others for who they are, but accept who you are first. Love unconditionally, stay in constant prayer. Assess why you want something before pursuing it. Remember that God is good all the time. God did and is continuing to do a work in and through you. Your life is a living testimony, so choose life and choose to live.

Marriage: You must compromise, humble yourself, and remember that your husband may not think or do things like you. You must communicate and be direct. Do not remain in an unhealthy relationship that may jeopardize your safety or that does not have hope. Never lose site of who you are in any relationship.

Children: Pray over your children often. Have faith, trust God and keep the lines of communication open. Teach your children about their bodies and what steps to take if they are violated.

<u>Pearls of Wisdom:</u>

• Continue seeking your happily ever after.
• When life happens, sometimes you have to pick up the pieces and start over.
• Looking for love in all the wrong places will not lead to happiness. Happiness begins from within.
• Suppressing your past hurt and pain can extend recovery time and delay healing and achieving happiness. You have to deal with your past in order to move forward into your future.
• When you hide or choose not to deal with your past or you deal with it by yourself, you are still being victimized by a particular person or situation by not being able to share your truth. Talk to God about what happened, how it affected you, and how you are feeling. Seek counseling so that you can talk about it to someone else and get help.
• You can't be concerned about how sharing your truth will affect others more than you are concerned with your own freedom and recovery.
• Do not let your own family dynamics of your youth affect the family dynamics of your adulthood. Be the change. Let it start with you!
• Alcoholism is real and it can affect so many areas of your life. You have to get help to overcome this addiction.

I OWN IT! SESSION:

1) Why do you think Mrs. Moving Forward ended up married to someone she loved but was not truly in love with?

2) In what ways have you looked for love in all the wrong places?

3) In what ways has this story inspired you?

4) Look up the following scriptures — 1 John 4:16 and Ephesians 2:4 — and correlate them to this story.

5) What level of persevering do you believe she is in?

Chapter 4
It Doesn't Matter How You Start, It Matters How You Finish

"Live your dreams, take risks, believe in yourself, have fun.
Do all things with love and remember the best is yet to come."

My name is Ms. Living The Life and this is my story. I am the youngest of four children. My parents' separated when I was about two years old and eventually divorced shortly thereafter. One of my siblings remembers our parents arguing a lot and one day our father left the house and he never came back. I never heard my mother talk badly about my father in front of us and I was too young to remember how life was with both of my parents together.

My immediate family is very close and we have always had each other's back. Growing up, I never felt alone. It is ironic that even though my siblings and I spend a lot of time together and we have a close relationship, I still feel that we are not emotionally connected to the point where we share our most intimate thoughts, events, and feelings. My mother raised us as a single parent and did a magnificent job. I always viewed my mother as a strong, independent and hardworking mother that went above and beyond to take care of her children. This shaped me to be a more independent woman as well, but it also made me less trusting of others. I developed the belief that I could not count on anyone else to do anything for me but me.

Growing up, I remember moving around a lot but I am unsure why. My mother believed in keeping the house very clean and organized. She made us clean the house from top to bottom and she was quick to wake us up if our chores were not completed or if we did not complete them satisfactorily to her liking. She was also one bossy lady. She was not an affectionate type of parent, but she focused more on parenting us, taking good care of us, working hard, and providing food on the table and shelter.

Even though my mother was all about her business, she was a very fun mother to have. She was always laughing, dancing, playing music, happy, and she worked out often. I use to go with my mother to work out at a young age and I really enjoyed it and that time I was able to spend with her. I still work out consistently to this day because of the example she set for me. She always kept herself together when stepping foot outside of the house. She taught us the importance of keeping ourselves up and looking nice. She worked a lot and was good at managing her money. We did not always have all the name brand clothes, but she kept us well dressed. I wouldn't ask my mother for things that I really desired to have because I saw how hard she worked to provide for us. I thought to myself, she probably cannot afford to get it anyway, so why bother to ask. I didn't want to stress her out trying to get things for me.

My mother got remarried when I was in the ninth grade, and I did not want her to marry my stepfather. She had dated another nice guy that lived with us for a period of time. He worked at General Electric and drove a glistening Mercedes-Benz and that is who I wanted my mother to marry. I thought if she married him, we would be rich. What I thought didn't matter because she married someone else. I viewed her new husband as mean and bossy. He would have a cow if we left the television on and we would find ourselves on punishment often for something simple like that. He did not seem loving to us and I argued with him all the time. I have a strong personality like my mother. I remember one of my friends had a great stepfather that seemed so nice and loving to her. Some of my other friends had their "real" biological father present in the household and active in their lives. I always felt like I missed out on that in my life.

As a child, I did not have a close relationship with my father. I could never rely on my father for much of anything. My father got remarried when I was in the first grade. I use to go occasionally to visit him and I always desired to have that special daughter/daddy time to spend with him alone. Well, that never happened for me. When I went to visit my father, I would stay with my stepmother and the children they had together, and I would most of time end up being their babysitter. I remember going over to his house in the summer to visit, taking care of my half siblings and always cleaning the house to my liking. I was a stickler for having a clean house because that is what I had grown accustomed to.

I never felt very comfortable around my father for some strange reason. I never got much attention from him and he never made me feel like I was special or loved. Sometimes he would not even show up when we were expecting him to come. As I got older, I began to resent him. He never called us for our birthdays; and when I did get the opportunity to talk to him, he didn't stay on the phone with me very long. He was not at my high school or college graduation, nor did he walk me or my sisters down the aisle when they got married. He let me and my siblings down repeatedly. All the feelings that I had internalized about my father for so many years finally began to surface and I was very disappointed and angry with him. As a result, I did not talk to my father for about two years. I was so over this ideal father I wanted him to be and I was so over him. When I finally reconnected with him, our relationship had not changed. Our relationship is just now improving within the past couple years or so since he has been sick and admitted back and forth to the hospital. It has taken my entire life for us to finally get closer and establish a real relationship. I talk to him frequently now and he even tells me that he loves me, which is something I always doubted. He has even joined a church, which is major because he never attended church before. My stepmother even apologized to me one day on his behalf for him not being there for me, for him not being an active part of my life, and for not being as responsible as he should have been.

My mother got pregnant at age seventeen and married very young. My two sisters got pregnant as teenagers too. I made up in my mind that I did not want to be a teenage mother and that I didn't want any babies. I desired to go to college. So my plan for my life was to finish school, get married and then begin having children by the age of twenty-five to twenty-seven. Because of the relationship I had with my father, I never felt loved by any man outside of being in an intimate relationship with them. I could not count on my father, therefore I felt like I could never depend on a man either. I believed that anything a man did for me was extra or a bonus. I always desired to get married, but at the same time, I have had a difficult time trusting men. This placed a major roadblock in my future plans of having a husband and family in my mid-twenties. I have a history of long-term relationships — one for eight years, one for two years, and another for ten years to someone I ended up marrying. My two previous relationships prior to getting marriage were pretty healthy, they just didn't result in marriage. One of the difficult parts of ending any relationship is when there are children involved and you get attached to them. The relationship that you have developed with the children ends too and that is disheartening. I kept telling myself that I didn't want to get involved with another man that had children, but that was a difficult task to accomplish and it limits your dating options.

The most difficult time in my life was my failed marriage. I got married at age thirty-two. We dated five years before getting married and were married for five years. Like my previous relationships, he too had children from a previous marriage. I felt like I gave all of myself in that relationship but got nothing in return. I felt very unappreciated in my marriage. One of the main problems in our marriage was my husband's ex-wife. She was the ex-wife but she had more control in our household than I did. She was very mean and negative, and it was her mission to treat me horribly every chance she got. She managed to brainwash the children and eventually turned them against me too.

My husband's family still invited her to many of the family gatherings. They were afraid that she would keep their grandkids away from them if they cut her off. I felt unimportant to my husband, the children, and most of his family. I made myself believe that when we got married things would change, but that was just wishful thinking. That never happened. My husband would never stand up for me or set boundaries with his ex-wife. Throughout the marriage, I could not help but feel I deserved more than I was getting. I was very unhappy most of the time and this was a very deep, dark time in my life. I felt like the kids didn't like me and I lived in a house full of people that were completely against me and truly didn't want me around. I was married but still felt alone the majority of the time. He paid his ex-wife child support even though the children were with us probably eighty-five percent of the time. There were times that we could not do certain things because their mother was supposed to come get them but would refuse to keep them. This was hard to understand and wrap my brain around. I was very miserable and each year my marriage continued to fall apart.

As I longed for love and attention from my husband, I ended up having an affair with someone else (who was also married) where I found some sense of peace and happiness. The affair made me feel free temporarily from my misery I was living in at home. It was entertaining to me, and the man I had an affair with thought the world of me. He said all the right things that I desired to hear. He treated me like VIP when we spent time together. When I was with him, I didn't think about what was going on around me. I just wanted to live in the moment. I didn't think about the consequences of having the affair at that time either. I just wanted a glimpse of happiness and a sense of feeling valued and appreciated.

I really regret having the affair at all, and I felt so much shame and condemnation. In the midst of the affair it felt so right, but in reality, I knew what I was doing was so wrong. Looking back on it, I wish I would have just decided to leave my husband instead of going the route of infidelity. I believe there is a big difference between a cheater and someone who cheats. A cheater is one who has it embedded within them. It is so natural for them to cheat. A cheater cheats more frequently, and it is most likely consistent in most, if not all, of their relationships. Someone who cheats may make a bad decision and cheat, but this may not be their normal character.

I personally enjoy being in a committed monogamous relationship, but I landed in the category of someone who cheated. My husband became suspicious and after some investigative work, he did discover that I was having an affair. We ended up separating. I moved out of our house and in with one of my friends for a little while. To cope with everything that was going on, I kept myself busy working and was hanging out with my good friends. During that time, I was not focused on my failing marriage at all. After about four months of that, I ended up moving back in with my husband to try to work on our marriage getting back on track. This lasted for about one year and still, nothing had changed or improved. I was still miserable and unhappy and everyone in the house felt the effects of my emotions. I was living a mediocre life. We even discussed the possibility of trying to have a baby, but in my heart, I knew that having a baby was not going to fix us. We eventually agreed that the marriage was not working out and it would be best for me to move back out and proceed with a divorce. So I moved out of the house again.

After I moved out, I was falsely accused of abandoning the family in spite of the fact that we agreed that this was the best decision and that I continued to assist with paying the bills for months after I left. I left my house and practically everything in it except my own personal belongings. Once I stopped contributing to paying the bills, he stopped letting me see the children. This made the ultimate lowest point in my life even more difficult. I was very depressed and I was uncertain as to what was in store for my future. I was not clear of my next move. I had lost myself somewhere along the way. At this point in time, I was alive but I had really stopped living. My life was in shambles. I thought to myself, if God can bring me through this, he can bring me through anything. I hated my life. I hated my job. And I hated myself for having the affair. I had to find a way to let go of the guilt of having this affair and get my life and myself together.

It was at that point that I knew I had to take back control of my life with God leading me every step of the way. I took a demotion and switched positions at my job because I was not satisfied with my current position. My mother and family were right there to support and encourage me during this difficult time in my life. There is nothing like a mother's wisdom and love. One day she sat me down and told me, "You do not have to live life unhappy. I left your dad and I had four children to care for and I made it through." It was at that very moment that I started living life for me. I found me a church home and got involved serving in it. I surrounded myself with my family and friends and I gained new friendships with positive individuals at church.

My relationship with God became closer and stronger than ever before. I prayed constantly. I had never prayed so hard in my entire life. I would wake up out of my sleep at night, mind racing, and I would begin to pray. I prayed for God to change my current situation and give me direction in my life. I prayed that he let me hear his voice and tell me what to do. I prayed at work. I prayed at home. "And pray in the Spirit on all occasions with all kinds of prayers and requests. With this in mind, be alert and always keep on praying for all the Lord's people." (Ephesians 6:18 NIV) I also had a circle of individuals praying for me, too. " For this cause we also, since the day we heard it, do not cease to pray for you, and to desire that ye might be filled with the knowledge of his will in all wisdom and spiritual understanding." (Colossians 1:9 KJV) After praying and thinking about what my mother said to me and how she made it through, I began to feel like I could make it through this, too. I began to see a light at the end of the tunnel and I began to have hope that my life would thrive again.

Going through this made me question a lot of things about myself. I felt like a failure because of my broken marriage. I questioned what was wrong with me. I asked myself, "Don't you want more for yourself than this?" I questioned whether I was lovable. I often wondered if my ex-husband married me just to have someone to help take care of his children. After all, I was the main one that took care of them, helped out financially, including paying their school tuition and child support, and the one doing the dropping off and picking them up from their activities. He was usually gone or working. Having had the affair was eating away at me, too. I was so disappointed in myself! I had to learn the concept of forgiveness. I had to forgive myself first, then others who had hurt me. I didn't know if I would ever find real love, get remarried, or have any children of my own. I had to take the necessary steps toward overcoming my insecurities and walk in my healing.

Life doesn't have to start off perfect for it to end up better. I didn't have the childhood that I wanted or desired. I didn't let it be the death of me nor did I let it keep me from continuing to work on improving myself, or work on my relationship with my father, or with others. Praying is a must. God may or may not change the situation we are in, but we can change the way we react to it or the way that we deal with it. Trust in God, he has a plan and it will work out the way he has intended. It may not seem like it sometimes during the process, but it will all work out. It may not be what we want or expect to happen, but we must trust God. Pray and ask God to take control and then let him. You can't just sit back and do nothing. I started being more obedient to his will in many areas of my life, like being a better steward of my money, studying the Bible more and practicing forgiveness. Sometimes I would pray for things I wanted, and when things didn't go my way I would get frustrated or mad. Then I would tell myself to snap out of it and get it together — and that would help me refocus and trust Gods plan.

Currently, I am living and enjoying life. I feel free. I do things I want to do and love to do. I am currently in a committed relationship with someone who supports and encourages me. He pushes me to be a better me. He is one of my biggest cheerleaders and he is always rooting me on. He doesn't want anything from me but love, support, quality time and commitment. He is financially stable and can take care of himself. I have been blessed to continue to meet some amazing new people that have become great friends. I have had several great job opportunities in my career. I travel the world and experience new things. I have a more open mind about many things including life in general. I am going places and doing things that I have never done or ever even dreamed of doing before. My mate is trustworthy and dependable. He shows me that he loves and appreciates me. I never thought I could or would be happy again but I am. At one time in my life, I was sure that I would be miserable forever but God had another plan for me. When I began to really pray and trust God, that is when things started to turn around for me. I began to see a glimpse of my happiness each day. I worked on discovering who I was as a person. I also received counseling from my pastor and linked up with other couples or people of faith who had been through the same or similar situations as I had gone through. I never gave up or gave in to the negative thoughts and feelings that were bouncing around in my head. Even after hitting rock bottom and experiencing some very challenging times when life happened to me, I persevered. If I did it, you can too. No matter what comes my way, I am determined to end strong!

Pearls of Wisdom:

- Every little girl needs a loving father to help navigate her through life and model what natural unconditional love looks like.
- When someone's biological father is absent, having a surrogate father figure or role model is vital to assist in the development of a young lady.
- Deal with any fears or insecurities related to yourself or relationships prior to entering into a new or serious relationship.
- Understand what love really is and what it means to you.
- Giving your all in a relationship can be a downfall if you are the only one giving and not receiving anything back in return.
- When outside influences (i.e., children, past relationships, exes, parents, friends) influence your relationship more than the two people involved, you run the high risk of relationship failure.
- Feelings of insecurity, lack of acceptance, lack of feeling appreciated coupled with other outside influences are explosive ingredients that can lead you to make bad choices and decisions that you may later regret. (i.e., infidelity, drugs/alcohol use/abuse, suicidal ideations, bad relationship choices, wrong life choices)
- Forgiveness is key! First, you have to forgive yourself and then forgive others that have wronged, hurt or disappointed you. Holding on to unforgiveness can destroy your life. (i.e., affect your health, torment your mind, stop your blessings, hinder your future)
- Pray hard like your life depends on it — because it does.
- Do not dwell in a state of self-pity.
- It doesn't matter how you start, it is how you finish that makes all the difference

I OWN IT! SESSION:

1) What challenges did Ms. Living the Life face?

2) Can you relate to this story in any way?

3) Do you see any similarities with this story and one of the other stories?

4) What helped these women persevere?

5) What are key points that you take away from this story?

6) Is it possible for a marriage to survive after infidelity, and if so, how?

7) What level of persevering do you believe she is in?

Chapter 5
The devil Tried It, BUT GOD

"Accept everything about yourself, I mean everything. You are YOU and that is the beginning and the end. No apologies, no regrets."

My name is Mrs. Survivor and this is my story. I was born and raised in Cincinnati, Ohio, and I am the youngest of four. I attended church as a little girl with my grandmother, but that subsided as I got a little older and stopped going on a regular basis. I was raised in a single parent home with my mom and my grandmother. My mom divorced my dad when I was about seven. I remember having somewhat of a good relationship with my dad and being a "daddy's girl" before the divorce, but after the divorce, our relationship went downhill.

My dad moved to another city and got remarried when I was about eleven or twelve years old. I would go there in the summers to visit my daddy in an attempt to try to rekindle our relationship, but that was an epic fail. I didn't really like his new wife at that time and I do not really even know why. I believe it had to do with this fairytale picture of my family, in my mind, of having my mother and father back together again. I felt as if my dad's wife was trying to take the place of my mom and I was not interested in that. My dad and I had a difficult time communicating with each other, so we barely could find the right words to say when we were together. I could not express my inner most feelings with my own dad because I really didn't know him well. Truthfully, my dad really didn't know me either. My efforts to rekindle our relationship were unsuccessful and did not last long. After two summers of going to visit him, I never returned thereafter. So I grew up without my dad being involved in my life.

In my teenage years, I was not really a social butterfly and I didn't have a whole lot of friends. I was picked on a lot because I was very skinny, nerdy, and I had bucked teeth. I always felt like I was ugly. I hated the way I looked and pretty much everything about myself. I hated my face, my nose, my hair, my teeth, how tall I was — everything. I wanted to look like the supermodels that I saw on television or the girls in the magazine. They were so beautiful to me. When it came to boys, I felt as if they didn't think I was cute enough. The boys really wouldn't talk to me or ask me out on dates. As a result, I had very low self-esteem, many insecurities and a difficult time loving myself. These feeling plagued my mind for years. Later in life, I began to gain too much weight, so I was still insecure with my body image and unhappy with myself and how I looked. Something had to change. I ended up attempting suicide because I always felt lonely and I felt like I just didn't belong. I was suffering from depression and I really needed some help to deal with this thing called life.

When I was about fourteen or fifteen, I was touched inappropriately by a family member, who needless to say is still around to this day. No one ever knew about it except my best friend at that time and my grandmother. I never told my mother about it because I knew if she knew, she would flip her lid and try to kill this individual. This molestation wasn't a long-term ordeal. As I recall, it only occurred a couple of times. After it happened, I stayed away for a very long time. When I can't deal with a situation or issue that is uncomfortable, I tend to stay away and bury it from my mind and suppress it. Now that I am older, seeing this person or thinking about what happened doesn't bother me at all. I have forgiven this person and have moved on past this situation. Each situation is different when it comes to anyone experiencing molestation/sexual abuse. I handled mine pretty much by myself. I believe that anyone who has or is experiencing any type of abuse should confide in someone they trust who can help them. Tap into resources available and seek professional counseling on how to handle and overcome this situation.

When I graduated from high school I actually decided to relocate about an hour away to where my dad lived to work on rebuilding my relationship with him. But my efforts were unsuccessful again. I eventually got involved in a relationship that seemed so right but ultimately led to being physically, mentally and emotionally abused. He was very controlling but at the same time, he took care of me and my needs. I thought I was in love and I thought he loved me. He controlled my every move. He controlled how long I was at the store, where I went, and who I spent time with. If I looked in the direction of another man, he would bite my head off or grab me up. He would also dictate what I could wear. I never wore makeup when I was with him so that it wouldn't be another issue to fight about. He constantly degraded me and always dug deep into my wounds of insecurities. He would state how big my nose was, how ugly I was and he often reminded me that no one would ever want me if I left him. As if that wasn't enough, he monitored my bathroom activities and my bowel movements too. I had difficulties with my digestive system and I wasn't going to the bathroom as much as he thought I should. He monitored my every move.

I became pregnant at the age of nineteen and had our son at twenty. He was abusive even during my pregnancy, with one episode resulting in me being thrown down a flight of stairs. Then he began to control how I raised our son. I continued to stay in this unhealthy relationship for about five years even though it was very abusive the whole time. I felt so helpless and I didn't feel strong enough to leave him, nor did I believe that I could live without him. I had always viewed my mother and grandmother as very strong women and I believe I inherited endurance from them, but I never viewed myself as that strong. I so wished I could be half as strong as they were when it came to difficult situations — especially this horrible situation that I found myself entangled in. I was terrified of this man but I was too afraid to leave. I was afraid of what he was capable of doing. He would usually apologize and tell me that he loved me and I would believe him. I wanted to believe that things would somehow, someday, change. I had convinced myself that there was no way of escape.

As time progressed, so did the abuse. Things did not get any better; they only got worse. The abuse became more frequent and more public. He began to be abusive in front of others including my mom. He started to become disrespectful to my family and I began to fear that he would hurt them too. I felt that I was putting my entire family in danger. I had finally reached my breaking point. I had made up in my mind that I was leaving this man after constantly thinking about it and contemplating it for years. I knew it was past time to leave. One night he asked me about getting married and having more children. I was honest with him and I told him I would never marry him or have any more children with him, ever. At that moment he punched me dead in my face. The next morning I dropped my son off at daycare and I went to work as I usually would. At work, I kept replaying all the aspects of our unhealthy relationship over and over in my head. I kept replaying what he did the previous night in my head and the conversation we had. I literally said to myself, "Bump this, I'm out!" I came to the realization that things were never going to change and I had had enough of this abuse. I could not and would not take it anymore. After work, I picked up my son from daycare and I jumped on the highway, 75 South, to go back home to where my family was. I finally left him! I did it! At that moment I realized that I was stronger than I ever imagined I was.

I stayed with my sister for about a week, hiding out. I didn't know what was going to happen next, so I had to come up with a game plan. Then I started getting death threats. I was afraid he was going to come looking for me and harm me and possibly my sister, so I felt as if I needed to get far away from him. I decided to head miles away from it all, so my mother put me and my son on a Greyhound and we went to go live in California with one of my family members. I lived there for about six months and things were cool there, but I was tired of hiding and running. I was homesick and I missed my family tremendously. I decided it was time to stop running, to face my fear head on and fight back. So we flew back home and lived with my mother for about six additional months. I found a new job and moved out into my own apartment. I also obtained a temporary protective order against him. It was time to move on with my life.

After I returned, little did I know I faced a new battle of fighting for custody of my son. He continued to try to exercise control over me and my life by trying to take my son away from me. I had countless court dates and I managed to rack up about $20K of my family's money on lawyers and court fees due to a long custody battle. During this time, I endured another two-plus year of emotional and mental abuse. At the end of it all, I won the court battle and was awarded guardianship of my son. I became a single mother and my son and his father never developed a close relationship. After I finally left him, I started rebuilding my life and working on me. I began experimenting with makeup, hairstyles, and various clothing styles. I began working at an insurance company and when I was eligible for dental insurance, the first thing I did was get braces to get my teeth fixed. I felt like I was finally in control of my life and I made my own decisions as it related to me and my son.

When I was about twenty-five years old, I met and married my first husband. I thought this was it. I was really in love now and we were going to make this last forever and live happily ever after. Well, guess what? That wasn't the case. My plans for my life just didn't seem to be working out as I had imagined they would. The first few years of being together and married were great, but he eventually introduced me to the nightlife, which was a lifestyle that I was not accustomed to. He loved to hang out on the town for entertainment. I never went out to clubs or did much of anything before I met him. Once he introduced me to the nightlife, I was eventually hooked and we started clubbing basically every single weekend of our entire marriage. He then turned me on to the strip clubs and eventually I started stripping too, and he was my "manager." I was working a full-time day job and began stripping at night. It took over our lives so much that we basically had an "open marriage." During this "open marriage," he had gotten another one of the strippers that we knew pregnant. My husband didn't have any children of his own when we met and I could not have any more children because I had a complete hysterectomy at the age of 28 due to female complications. At the time that he had gotten this other woman pregnant, we were separated but still legally married. He began to treat me horribly.

I was living in an efficiency apartment with my son who was gone with his father for a visit one lonely day. I wanted to reconcile things with my husband and I tried to talk to him about our marriage. The tone in which he spoke to me and yelled at me made me feel inadequate and it felt as if I wasn't good enough for him anymore or anyone else for that matter. At that moment, I felt worthless. This triggered old feelings and insecurities that I had felt from my past and my previous abusive relationship. I do not like conflict and confrontation, so when I have to face these feelings head on, I cannot cope and then I just shut down. Finding out about this pregnancy with another woman along with my failing marriage took me over the edge. I decided to end it all. I was not interested in partaking in this thing called life any longer. I took a bunch of pills, cried my heart out and lay down on my couch to die. All of a sudden I heard a strange voice speaking very clearly to me, which I now know was God, and the voice said, "Do not do this. Get up and call for help!" I immediately got up and called the poison control center for help. They immediately advised me to go to the hospital and I did. That was one of the worse experiences of my life because I had to have my stomach pumped, and then I stayed at the hospital on a thirty-six-hour suicide watch in the psychology unit. I could have ended it all. What about my son? What about my family and those individuals who truly loved me? I didn't think about how my suicide would have changed and affected their lives too. I was only thinking of myself and ending temporary (but what seemed like permanent) pain. After this ordeal, I knew it was time for a major change. I was married for about 5 ½ years total. I initiated and proceeded with the divorce without hesitation, and it was a lot easier to leave this time than it was before. In the past, I lived a life that was pleasing to others, but it was time for me to really live my life for me. I started going to Women Helping Women and attended group counseling to get my life together.

"The thief cometh not, but for to steal, and to kill, and to destroy: I am come that they might have life, and that they might have it more abundantly" (John 10:10 KJV)

I remained single for about two years and then I met someone new. After some time we began dating seriously. We dated for two years and ended up getting married and he is now my husband of eight years. I am happy and my marriage is healthy. I am a more confident person now than I have ever been before. Do not get me wrong, I still struggle with some insecurities at times, but it's not nearly as bad as it used to be. My husband tells me every single morning how beautiful I am and how much he loves me. As good as that sounds, there is still something within me (due to my past experiences) that has to believe it completely and stop believing the lies of the enemy. I have battled post-traumatic stress disorder and depression over the years. I have taken many steps to improve my life, myself as a person, and I am working on living fearlessly while overcoming my past. I am much healthier now mentality and physically.

One day I made a choice to lose some weight because I was so uncomfortable with the extra pounds that I had put on over the years. I began to work out consistently, lift weights, and eat healthier. I was able to meet my goal of losing weight and I began to tone my body and build muscle. I am now healthy and the most physically fit than I have ever been in my entire life. My weight loss journey has motivated and inspired many people to become healthier and I have been featured throughout social media sites for my fitness accomplishments. I am now modeling; I am a figure competitor and a personal trainer. Who would have ever imagined an ugly duckling like me would be in a position to do the things that I am doing today? God! That is who, because HE always knew. To keep myself on the right track, I try to keep positive people in my inner circle. I read positive quotes often. I read scriptures from the Bible, and even talking about my past life's experiences has been therapeutic for me. I am working on increasing my faith and renewing my spiritual and mental being.

My advice to the readers who have faced similar experiences as mine would be to seek individual and group counseling, get a life coach who can help mentor you and help you stay focused on how to overcome life challenges that you may face. If anyone is in an abusive relationship, get out of it. Devise an escape plan, follow through with the plan, and don't turn back. I am so thankful that I am not in that abusive relationship today. If I had stayed in that abusive relationship many years ago, who knows if I would still be alive to tell my story today. I use to think I wouldn't make it in life without my son's father, but I did indeed make it without him and I am in a better head-space. You can make it without "him" too. If I had of ended my life after more than one attempt, I would not be here making an impact on others today. I am not perfect, nor have I been completely healed from my past. I continue to have fears and struggles today. I'm still a work in progress even after being remarried. I have overcome some major hurdles in my life and in spite of not having it all figured out, I am persevering. Today, I am a much better version of me than I have ever been and I refuse to go back to who I use to be. Through it all, I am a survivor!

Pearls of Wisdom:

• With your own strength, you only have a limited amount of power to overcome, but with a relationship with God, a spiritual foundation, spiritual guidance, and a positive mindset, you have unlimited power to overcome anything and expedite your complete healing.

• It is important as a young child to start to identify who you are and love who God created you to be.

• Develop and continue to revive your own self-love and self-actualization.

• Having low self-esteem can result in less favorable decision-making and behavior.

• Never compare or compete with another person but self.

• Celebrate the greatness in you and those things that you appreciate in others.

• Do not allow your circumstance to define you. You define it and own it.

• Once you build a high level of self-confidence and self-esteem, then it will be easier to identify what your passion and purpose is.

• If you struggle with self-esteem issues, seek God for protection, strength, and direction so that you will not fall prey to the tricks and attacks of the enemy (i.e., suicidal ideations/attempts, depression).

• You are stronger than you think you are. Make yourself a priority and do what is best for you.

I OWN IT! SESSION:

1) Read Romans 12:1-2 and write how it would relate to Mrs. Survivor.

2) What other scriptures come to mind when reading this story?

3) In what ways did Mrs. Survivor persevere?

4) Are you or someone you know in an abusive relationship? Is there an exit plan?

5) What type of support would be helpful to someone in an abusive relationship?

6) What level of persevering do you believe she is in?

Chapter 6
My Pain Has Purpose

My name is Ms. Victorious and this is my story. I am the oldest of five children that grew up in a single-parent household. My mother raised us pretty much by herself and we were extremely close. Even though my dad was not actively involved in raising us, I was a major "Daddy's girl" and I loved my daddy. I would visit him when my siblings would refuse to. One time when I got mad at my mother, I called myself grown enough to choose to go live with my dad. Well, that did not last long and I was right back with my rock, my dear mother. I know internally she knew it would be a matter of time before I would come running back home, but she let me go and experience life for myself. I was like a mother figure to my other siblings because I was the oldest, so I tried hard to keep them all in line and at the same time tell them what to do or not to do. I was the "BOSS," outside of our mother of course, and I gave orders well.

I would say that I am an introvert. I can be shy and quiet until you get to know me. I never liked to be the center of attention and I enjoyed spending time alone. I never was the type that liked to go out much and hang out in the clubs or parties. I would hang out with a couple of my friends occasionally, but for the most part, you would find me at work, church, with family, or in the bed. I LOVED MY BED! I was never interested in being popular or hanging with the in-crowd. I knew I stood out. I was definitely different. Smoking or drinking was never my thing either, but a "sista" loved to throw down on some good old soul food. My mother was born down South in the country with the deep red dirt roads, so I was exposed to some good cooking and eating by her, my grandmother and my aunts. I would rather get me a good plate of food, lie down in my bed and watch some good old country western or sci-fi flicks and I would be good to go.

I always desired to get married and have children but that never happened for me. God obviously had other plans for me. I had a couple of marriage proposals in my life, but I was a woman who refused to settle for less than what I desired and deserved for myself, which was the best. If you came for me, you had better come correct or not at all. So as I waited on God to send me my husband, I resided with my mother. My sister would often tease me, asking if I thought my husband was just going to come knocking on my door or window because I didn't do much to meet anyone. She often wondered if I did get married, would I move him in the house with my mother or was I going to finally move out to my own place? I didn't have an answer for that question because I was unsure myself. I wasn't going to even worry about the living arrangements until that time came to get married and decide. I was preparing to one day move out on my own whether I got married or not. I bought a variety of household items and I stored them in a closet in anticipation for when that big day came. That day never came for me.

Although I wasn't blessed with my own child, I had the privilege of obtaining custody of my niece and raising her. Since I didn't have any children of my own, this was a challenging experience, but I had my mother there to help guide me. Raising a child is a tough job, especially when it is not your biological child. But I loved her as if she was my own. I was very strict on her, but it was because of my old school values and beliefs and also I wanted the very best for her. I wanted her to stay focused on school so that she would be well rounded, educated and successful as an adult. I also wanted to protect her from all the evils of this world. I was placed in this position unexpectedly with no time to plan or prepare to be a mother figure to anyone. I know I had always desired it, but what did it consist of. God has a funny way of giving you what you ask for, but it may be in a different form than you expect. I did not always make the right decisions as it related to raising her, but I did my best to raise her in a good environment, protect her and provide for her needs. It would have been nice to have a parenting manual or a golden rule handbook that helps you raise children. We can rely on the Holy Spirit and the Bible to be our teacher but it was not a cake walk. I did the best I was capable of doing. My main goal was to get her through high school and to graduate with no babies. My mission was accomplished. My other nieces and nephews would frequently spend the night or live with us. My mother and I were a good team that joined together in an effort to raise all of the little ones. Although they would get into my things and wear on my last nerves, I truly loved them all.

I am the type of person that loves hard and will try to help and be there for others whenever I can. When I didn't feel that in return or felt unappreciated, it was a hard pill to swallow. I would cut you off in an instant if I felt the need to. I sometimes struggled in this area and would have a hard time forgiving others and letting things go. When someone would hurt me, it cut me deep within and my scars would take a while to heal. Forgiveness is a very difficult thing to master, but it is so necessary. "But if you do not forgive others their sins, your Father will not forgive your sins." (Matthew 6:15)

My first love is God. I have loved God with ALL of my heart and soul for a long time. God is my everything. Although I am not perfect, I have strived to live my life according to God's purpose and plan for me. I have tried to be an example for others that I encountered. I not only attended church, I tried to live according to God's will and treat people well. I received great joy from being able to minister to others and serve at church. My walk with God is solid and I would never trade it for anything. Choosing God was the best thing that I have ever done. I am so thankful that he chose me first, loved me unconditionally, and he never gave up on me. Even through those difficult times in my life, I knew HE was right there for me to see me through.

My life changed forever when I was diagnosed with cancer. Ironically, I had taken out a cancer life insurance policy not very long before I began getting sick. I have always been there for my mother and I worried about her and if she would be okay if something was to happen to me. I didn't want to die and leave those I loved so much behind. I prayed and hoped for a miracle. I didn't know or understand why this was happening to me, but I needed God's strength to get me through it. I thanked God for every additional month and day that I was still in the land of living on this side. I had to fight with every fiber of my being to live. Each year I was still on this earth, I counted a blessing. The little stuff that consumed me before didn't seem so important anymore. There are so many things that I still want to do and several places that I still want to go. Through all the appointments, treatments and pain, every moment was precious to me. I had to go through a boatload of tests, doctor's appointments, medication changes, surgeries/procedures and chemotherapy.

Along with this disease came body image changes too. I lost a lot of weight for the first time in my life but then I became insecure with the extra flabby skin especially on my arms. Some days I felt okay and other days the chemo made me feel horrible. My appetite was poor most days. Food didn't taste near the same anymore. I was super sensitive to many things like metals and hot/cold temperatures. My eating habits changed. My energy level changed. My sleeping pattern changed. My entire life began to change right before my eyes. I only wanted a few people to know what I was going through and I asked them not to tell anyone. I wanted to deal with this in my own personal way and I did not need sympathy from others. It was a huge pill to swallow and I didn't want everyone to worry about me. Through it all, I knew God was in control, and he had the final say on when my life would end on this side of the earth and when my eternity would begin. I am a daughter of the King. My God has the perfect plan for me.

After a few years of fighting and battling this awful, hateful, life-altering disease, God called my name and I transitioned to my new home. When someone dies from this illness, some people say that the person lost their battle with cancer while other people say that the person won their battle with cancer. Some people say that when someone passes away from a dreadful disease such as this that they are now healed. I guess it is a matter of perspective. I hated to leave my family that I loved so dearly to the end of the earth, but when it is your time, it is your time to go. It is true that I have been temporarily separated from some of my family that is near and dear to my heart, but I believe there is no greater love than the love of our creator God. God showed me the place that He had prepared for me a few years before I was diagnosed with cancer and passed away. God told me not to worry about anything because He had thought of everything that I could ever even think of or imagine, that he had it all worked out and taken care of — and he did. Whether I lost or won my battle with cancer does not matter to me because I won over the adversary and I gained my crown. I am no longer in pain. I am no longer battling cancer or any other disease now. I no longer have to take medicine or chemotherapy. I am in a better place, so I am a winner.

I had my life all planned out too, with so many hopes and dreams. My life threw me a lot of detours, roadblocks and stop signs, but I kept on living. At the end of the day, I lived the life that God had planned for me. I hope I fulfilled my purpose on this earth. We never know when it is our time to leave this world and enter into eternity. We have to live life to the fullest today and every day. Live your life with purpose and be intentional about everything. Make it a mission of yours to make a difference in the life of someone else. Follow your dreams and walk into your destiny. Even though throughout my life many things did not go as I planned and I had several challenges to face, my hardest battle was to fight to actually live. Through my battle, I persevered! Since I am no longer here to tell my story, a couple of people that were a part of my life will complete my story and tell you what they think of me.

Servant of God:

I call her servant of God. I met Ms. Victorious around July in the year 2000 when she and her mother were in Mississippi. We were first cousins but we had never met before. Her father was my uncle, but the strangest part of it was that I never knew that he even existed. She came to visit with my mother and I just happened to be in town at the same time for a family get together and I am so thankful that I was there to meet her and discover some truths regarding my family. She resembled one of my younger sisters, so I knew instantly that we had to be family. We immediately connected and exchanged contact information to keep in touch. We did just that too because we had years upon years of catching up to do. We lived in two different states but we began communicating at least once or twice a month over the phone. I really enjoyed getting to know her and talking to her.

We always had good conversations but she was a very private person and she did not gossip about others. She would never reveal to me her age, so all I knew is that she was born in March and my birthday was the day after hers. I did learn that she loved going to church, she loved helping people, and she LOVED God and her family. I could tell from our conversations that she was heavily involved in the church and she was very family oriented. She spent a lot of time working, usually two jobs and taking care of her mother. She didn't talk to me about marriage or her relationships, and I didn't pressure her to tell me anything too personal. I enjoyed hearing about the areas of her life that she did let me in on.

She constantly invited me to visit her and I had planned to take her up on that offer so that we could spend some more time together. But I kept putting it off and that opportunity never came.

She appeared to be the type of person that was easy to get along with, but she did not desire to have a close association with that many people. Besides working a lot, she didn't seem to do any hanging out. She was secure with having a small circle of family and friends that she was very close with and that she loved dearly. She would do anything to help and care for those individuals in that circle. They were her world. I loved and admired that about her. She was such a great person and I was proud to have a cousin like her.

I was in shock when I got the call that she had passed away. I felt a little betrayed because as close as we were she didn't even tell me that she was sick. She didn't inform me of what she was going through. I would have loved to have known and been there for her during that difficult time in her life. Knowing the person she was, I do somewhat understand why she didn't tell me though. I can't begin to imagine what frame of mind she was in from shock to pain, to agony, to fear, to denial on top of trying to cope with everything going on with her and around her. Sometimes I would call her but she wouldn't answer or if she did she would just tell me she wasn't feeling well and she would call me later. I assumed that it was just a temporary illness and she would be back to her normal self in no time. She never complained either. She was fighting for her life and I did not have a clue what she was going through. I should have known something was wrong when she was not working like she was accustomed to doing. I just thought she was laid off work or taking a break from working so much. I would never have imagined she was battling cancer or that she was so sick. I wish I could have been there for her like she always was for others. I never even had the opportunity to say good-bye.

My favorable memories of Ms. Victorious are all good ones. She was a great person with a good soul and a heart for helping people. She was very instrumental in me getting to know more of my family, including her dad/my uncle. Meeting her has changed my life completely. People tend to stress over things like bills, their children, their jobs, etc. …Those things will be here when we leave this world. We may or may not be able to change certain things in our lives, but we cannot stress over it and let it get the best of us. She was and still is such an inspiration to me. I tend to believe her work here on earth was not done but just getting started. There are people here on earth that still need her and could benefit from knowing her. She was an ambassador that represented a loving spirit. There was nothing that she wouldn't do for you if she was able to do it. She was a direct person, but kind and gentle at the same time. I am positive that whoever crossed her path was blessed by her and inspired.

Getting sick put her on a new path. She didn't focus on herself even during her illness. Instead of being selfish, she was a selfless person who performed selfless acts for others. Even through her illness, she was concerned about protecting others from worrying about her. She was very skilled and tactful in communicating. She downplayed her pain and illness very well. She kept going until she just couldn't go anymore. She was literally a saint in my eyes. She was resilient in spite of everything she was going through. When I became very ill myself, after she had already passed away, I wasn't sure if I would make it through my battle. But I would think of her and her strength and I got the will to keep on fighting through it. Because she persevered, she helped me and still is helping me to persevere too.

Virtuous Woman:

I call her Virtuous Woman. When I think of Ms. Victorious, I think of Proverbs 31. "Who can find a virtuous woman? For her price is far above rubies." (Proverbs 31:10) She was a virtuous woman and her price was far above rubies. She was a person of righteousness who always tried to do good and always saw the good in others. She was a very hard worker. I worked with her for many years and she hardly ever missed a day of work. You had to be strong to survive at our job and that is why she made it. She was a very strong person to me. She was stronger than she ever even knew, I believe. Some thought she was weak and they thought she would not last there at that job. She proved them all wrong. One guy, in particular, would always pick at her and try to get her to break. It took physical and mental strength to survive that. I never understood how she did it. There were a few days when I would see the tears wail up in her eyes — but she just kept going. I remember walking over to her and placing my hand on her shoulder and reassuring her that everything would be all right. It was at that moment that I realized that those were not tears of fear but tears of determination to fight her way through the challenges that surrounded her and those were the days that she showed the most strength.

Sometimes I believe you have to get to a place of being uncomfortable and fed up in order to be pushed forward to get to where you need to be. She would always remind me, "What won't kill me, will make me stronger!" Then she would do her walk of faith and sway her hips back and forth and tell me to look at her while she would shimmy on down the walkway with confidence. Then she would do an about-face or a 360-degree turn and beckon for me to look again as she shimmied back toward me. Of course, I would be in stitches laughing hysterically at her. She was such a funny person and I spent many days laughing at and with her, which made those difficult days in my life much easier to bear.

She was such a great person to know. I saw so many different sides to her. I saw her when she was happy, especially at the end of the workday when it was time to go home. She would almost run everyone over to get out of that place! I had fun riding behind her as she drove wildly out of the parking lot and onto the highway. She would drive like "The Fast and the Furious" and would get us to our exit real quick. I also saw her on sad days while having to deal with a mean co-worker who just didn't know how to stop running his big mouth and stop when enough was truly enough. He would really try to bring her down and mess with her for no reason at all. Every now and then, I got to see that angry side of her come out and strike back too. He never even took the time to get to know her for the wonderful person she was. He had no idea who he was really messing with. She usually came to work with a smile on her face and to see her happy was such a delight. When she would frequently talk about her "Pooh" her face would just light up the room. She enjoyed talking and sharing different stories about him. I was glad she had him in her life. Knowing that she never had any kids of her own, at least she had her nephew that she was so close to, to love on like her own. I could she loved him to the moon and beyond.

Ms. Victorious was a giver. If you didn't have lunch for the day, she would offer you some of what she had without hesitation. She was also an encourager. She was more than a co-worker to me; she was a great friend and good person to talk to. She never made me feel uncomfortable about sharing anything with her. She was someone I could just open right up to and feel like it was okay to do so. She was someone I could truly confide in. She was someone who would help lift up my spirits when I was having a rough day. I know she was not perfect, but I never saw any wrong with her. I really admired her and looked up to her. It was hard to lose her because when I did, I lost a special friend. I was there by her side at the very moment she took her last breath. Her death was the hardest that I have faced thus far. I never understood why she had to die so soon and especially that way. Her passing has made an imprint on my brain that I will never forget. I will never forget her or that day she left this earth.

Shortly after she passed away, my great grandmother was placed in a nursing home and she wanted me to choose some things from her house that I wanted. One of the things that I chose was an African-American angel figurine and I named it after my dear friend. I know she is watching over me right now as I am reflecting on her story and her life. She is my angel and she meant so much to me, probably more than she ever knew. Thank you for being a good friend to me and impacting my life in more ways than you could ever imagine. You are a great example of the word "persevere." I love you and you will be in my heart forever. Until we meet again…

"Nothing can dim the light that shines from within"

Pearls of Wisdom:

• Live everyday as if it is your last day because you do not know when that last day will come.

• Do not worry about what you do not have, but instead focus on what you do have.

• Never forget how blessed you really are.

• Strive to make an imprint on someone else's life today and every day.

• Be a doer, Be a giver, Be a FIGHTER.

• Find your God-given purpose in life and walk in it.

I OWN IT! SESSION:

1)   If someone who has cancer dies, do you think they lost or won their battle with it and why?

2)   How are you making an impact in someone else's life and/or in society?

3)   How will you begin or continue to live your life to the fullest?

4)   What do you think others will say about you when you are gone?

5)   What scriptures come to mind when reading this story?

6)   In what ways did Ms. Victorious persevere?

7)   What level of persevering do you believe she is in?

Chapter 7
I Don't Look Like What I Have Been Through

"My mission in life is not merely to survive, but to thrive; and to do so with some passion, some compassion, some humor, and some style" –Maya Angelou

My name is Mrs. I'm Still Standing and this is my story. I grew up in a single-parent household and I too became a single mother for several years. Life for me has not gone at all how I had planned. I struggled with low self-esteem as a child and through young adulthood. I have struggled financially to make ends meet. I have experienced a great deal of loss in my past and I have battled situational depression. I have been through many tests, trials and storms. Life has not been easy for me and I have had to fight my way through in many areas of my life. Yes, I have made some poor choices, bad decisions, and mistakes along the way. Through all of my ups and downs, with God by my side, I have made it through and I am still standing to tell my story.

I am the baby of the family, but do not for one minute think that I have been spoiled rotten, because I wasn't. That is so far from the truth in my situation. In fact, I have oftentimes felt like the oldest child in many ways, and when difficult decisions arise, I am called upon to come to the rescue, come up with the answers and solutions. So being a spoiled brat even for one day would be a great idea to entertain. My parents divorced when I was very young and my mother was awarded custody of the children. I resided with her and we remained in the house where I grew up. As a result, I am a product of living in a single-parent household. This was my mother's second go around at marriage, which eventually lead to divorce number two. I was so young when my parents were together that I cannot recollect what it was like living as a family with my father in the house with me on a day-to-day basis. My new normal was living with my mother and siblings and visiting with my dad at another location. Would this be called my second home or just a place where my father resides and I just came to visit every now and then? It makes me believe that I had envisioned what life was like living in a two-parent home with my mother and father and what marriage looks like.

In my eyes, my perception of living in a single-parent home meant that funds were limited, which limited what I could have. As a child, you want everything you see and you expect your parents to provide it. Now do not get me wrong, my mother took great care of us. She kept us clean and nicely dressed; she kept our hair combed/cut; we had home-cooked meals; the house was always nice and clean, and she made sure that we attended school and did not miss unless absolutely necessary. She focused on making sure we had everything we needed and not everything we wanted or asked for. I might not have had all the name brands clothes that I wanted, but I had enough cute clothes to wear every day. We tend to take simple things for granted in life and as a child, you may not always understand the significance of having your basic needs met. It is when you realize that the norm for someone else may be less favorable that you learn to appreciate your situation more. I grew up in the suburbs and through my eyes, all my friends grew up with a similar lifestyle as mine and some with a much better lifestyle than mine. Some of my friends had both their parents in their home and some didn't. It seemed like my friends that had both parents lived better than I did. They seemed to always have all the latest and greatest fashions, nice cars, nice parties, the cutest hairstyles, and everything else a child desired. I sometimes thought to myself, "if my mother and father were still together, I could live that way too."

Looking back as a mother and as an adult now, I see that the reality is that you cannot buy your child everything they want or ask for whether there are one or two parents in the home when you budget and spend money wisely. In some cases, it may be true that having a two-parent household may allow you to do more for your children, but there are so many factors that can affect that such as the family size, the household income, the number and amount of household bills, and their spending habits to name a few. You don't think of how much money is spent on bills to maintain the household as a child, but when you grow up and reality soon sets in, you begin to learn about the responsibilities of maintaining a household. I am thankful that because I didn't get everything I wanted, I lived with the security of knowing I was going home to a clean house with dinner on the stove, lights on, and a home phone. Things could have been a whole lot worse. My life was good and I didn't even know it!

My mother was a phenomenal woman who raised five children on a "fixed income" as she always called it. She injured her back on her job so she was unable to work a significant portion of her life. My mother loved to dress up in her fancy clothes with her hats, purses and shoes to match. Whenever she stepped foot out of the house, she made sure everything was in the right place and that she was looking good. Her passion was cooking, and planting a flower and vegetable garden every year. She served as a "Mother" and Evangelist in the church for years. She also served on the prison ministry in which she would take cookies to the inmates and she would talk, encourage and pray with them. She was a Sunday School teacher and she also prepared and preached several sermons. She was bold and feisty and she wasn't afraid to minister to anyone, including family, friends, and strangers. She was the type of person who always could tell if something was going on with you without you saying a word. She was a blessing to many people who met her.

In my heart, I have always longed to be a daddy's girl. It is funny because even though I had a closer relation with my mother than my father, one day my mother said to me, "You have always been a daddy's girl." That was shocking to me when she said that because I didn't think in my mind that I acted in this way nor did I ever dare say that to her. Mothers know it ALL. When you have that maternal instinct and a personal relationship with God, there is a lot that you discover without it being seen or verbally said. My mother knew many of my most unspoken but deepest desires. I lived in a separate household, but I still saw my father and I remember going to visit with him and staying for a few days before returning home. I have to admit I loved visiting with my father because I got to pick out what I wanted to eat. I remember being able to pick Fruit Loops or Apple Jacks cereal for breakfast and thinking this is living the life. I remember going to McDonald's, sleeping until I wanted to get up and watching whatever I wanted on the television. I had more choices and more freedom when I was with him. I don't think we followed a visitation schedule because I do not remember going over to his house during the week for a few hours every week or regularly on the weekends. When my parents got a divorce, I doubt if they even had a set visitation schedule then. So these visits seemed to be scattered here and there while growing up but whenever they came, I was excited about it. As a child, it was just the little things that made you bubble over with joy and be on cloud nine.

I remember when my birthday or Christmas would come around, my father would ask me what I wanted for my present and I would run down the list to him. This was my opportunity to think big, so I would ask for things that I knew my mother was probably not going to get. I specifically remember asking for some name brand jeans like Jordache, Calvin Klein, Guess and some Gloria Vanderbilt because I wanted to be in style and rock the latest fashions that I felt like everyone else was wearing. When the time came and I would get my special gifts, I would eagerly open the box to see if I got what I asked for. And guess what? I opened the box to find just what I asked for. I was the happiest girl in the world and I felt like I had the best dad in the world because he would get me whatever I would ask for and I could go to school and rock my new stylish Jordache, Calvin Klein's and Gloria Vanderbilt jeans. Days like these, life was good.

Looking back at this time in my life, it reminds me of how God desires our relationship with HIM to be. We should go to our Father, think big, and take the limits off. John 14:13-14 (NIV) says, "And I will do whatever you ask in my name, so that the Father may be glorified in the Son. You may ask me for anything in my name, and I will do it." Just like I thought my earthly father was all that and a bag of chips, I have to view my Heavenly Father like that and even greater. In Psalms 37:4 (NIV) it says, "Take delight in the Lord, and he will give you the desires of your heart." It has taken me a long time, a lot of life experiences, and many sleepless nights to come to the realization that I serve a limitless God. If I had applied that same faith that I had as a child toward my earthly father (when I asked for my "big" special gifts and believed that I would get them) to the faith I have had in my Heavenly Father (God) over the years, my oh my, dealing with life and the storms that come, and the test and trials that I have faced would have been much easier to bear. In Job 11:7-9 (NIV) it reminds us of how incredible our God is. "Can you fathom the mysteries of God? They are higher than the heavens above- what can you do? They are deeper than the depths below- what can you know? Their measure is longer than the earth and wider than the sea." I am learning each day to not just say it but truly take the limits off of my GOD. As my relationship deepens with God, I fall deeper in love with HIM and appreciate HIM more and more. Now with confidence, I can truly say, "I AM A DADDY's GIRL" for my Heavenly Father is so amazing to me!

Hopes and Dreams

I longed for my parents to get back together. In my mind, just maybe one day, one day, they would remarry and we would be one big happy family. What I didn't know is what caused them to get divorced in the first place. I really didn't care what the cause of the divorce was either. I was only concerned with having my parents together. I held on to this dream as long as I could. My dream was partially shattered after a visit with my father at his house and I found a woman's robe in his bathroom. "What in the world is this?" I thought. "Who is this "mystery" woman?" I didn't know he was dating someone and I have never seen nor met another woman outside of my mother. There were no other signs of a woman living there with him, but clearly, someone was in the picture and comes to visit. I never mentioned it or asked my father about it. He probably wouldn't tell me much anyway. Even though I don't remember, I am pretty sure I told my mother when I got home. I was devastated and I felt a sense of disappointment. My father has a girlfriend or someone special in his life. I began to think, "Maybe they will not get back together after all."

I never saw my mother date either. Men were not coming in and out of our household unless they were truly a family member or we needed something on the house repaired or remodeled. There were no live-in boyfriends, no new uncles that I never met before, or a new boyfriend every other week. There was not late night rendezvous or overnight outings. It was as if my mother had no desire for my father or any other man for that matter. I knew that men were interested in her, but she did not pay them any mind or give them the time of day. At least she didn't in front of me anyway. She seemed content with being alone. When I became an adult, my mother would share bits and pieces of stories here and there that made me see that she had her own personal reasons for filing for divorce and not looking back. I wanted to hear it but at the same time, I didn't want to hear anything bad about my daddy.

My dream of my parents getting back together was fully shattered and broken into a million pieces when I was in junior high/high school. That's when I was informed my father was getting remarried to someone else. Oh, no! This can't be so! Who in the world is my father marrying and is this the mystery woman whose robe was in my father's bathroom? The reality of no reunion for the two of them was clear. Then to top it off, I was in the wedding. So I had to grin and bear it all. Well, I guess it was time to come up with a new dream because the old one was soon to be null and void. My last hope was if they both magically had a change of heart and decided they could no longer live without each other. Well, that never happened either.

So I cooperated and went along with the whole wedding ordeal against my will and my heart. I was in my father's wedding but my guards were up to the tenth power. I had built a wall up and I was not going to let his wife in. I had a mother already, so there was no need to have two. My father belonged with my mother not another woman in my eyes and that is how it was all supposed to be in my youthful mind. I had to be there to support him — after all, he was my "daddy" — and I couldn't let him down. I had to pretend like all was okay and I was not fazed by any of this. To be honest, no one asked me how I felt about the divorce, this new woman, or the new marriage and wife. Did anyone care what I thought about it all? Do children have a voice or a say so in the matter at all? The truth is, I kept my hopes and dreams of my parents remarrying to myself and they never knew how much I was consumed with the idea.

Since the walls went up early in the relationship, I never developed a close relationship with his new wife. I tolerated her and respected her as my father's wife, but she was not my mother or nothing like the mother that I was accustomed to. Not that she was a bad person or mother, I just wasn't ready to truly accept her or this change. I didn't allow myself to let her into my world or love her completely, and I didn't feel that she let me in hers either. I am sure she felt the resistance, but she didn't say anything or seem to care. Maybe if she had done more to tear down the wall between us as the adult, we could have really taken the time to personally get to know each other and develop a strong relationship. I didn't feel that motherly love from her and she would introduce me as my father's daughter and not her daughter or stepdaughter. That always made me feel like she just tolerated me, but I continued to respect her and kept it moving. If I had looked at things with a more positive perspective, I could have had the best of both worlds. I mean think about it, how cool is it to have two mothers? Well, since I was feeling some type of way, this was my new normal now, so we both tolerated each other and were cordial to each other in this new situation. Besides, it wasn't like I lived with them or we had to see each other on a frequent bases. We never gave each other a chance to really get to know each other or develop into what could have possibly been a good, healthy relationship. Since I didn't have the best relationship with her, I allowed it to affect my relationship with my father as an adult. To avoid being around her, I sometimes stayed away from my father. That is one thing I regret doing to this day. I can never get that time back.

My father moved out of his house and into the house with her. It was a bigger house than he had and I still went to visit and spent the night occasionally. The visits did become farther apart and I did not see or talk to my father as much anymore. I felt like his new wife was taking my father away from me. This is a horrible thing to feel as a child. This made me resent her even more. "Why wouldn't she want her husband to spend time with his children and try to get to know me better?" I thought, Since I had no say so, I would just enjoy anytime I could with him. All kinds of things were running through my youthful head. I now know that when your head is racing with all types of beliefs and even negative thoughts or perceptions, the enemy will have a field day making the situation seem even bigger and worse than it probably is or has to be. His sneaky self will be delighted to play on your emotions and cause even more division in your family. Romans 12:1-2 (MSG) says: "So here's what I want you to do, God helping you: Take your everyday, ordinary life–your sleeping, eating, going-to-work and walking-around life–and place it before God as an offering. Embracing what God does for you is the best thing you can do for him. Don't become so well adjusted to your culture that you fit into it without even thinking. Instead, fix your attention on God. You'll be changed from the inside out. Readily recognize what he wants from you, and quickly respond to it. Unlike the culture around you, always dragging you down to its level of immaturity, God brings the best out of you, develops well-formed maturity in you." Because I became adjusted to this new culture and new negative thinking, I let it get the best of me. Remember, my desire always was to be a daddy's girl, but after he got remarried, it drove us farther apart.

I do remember going out of town with my father and his wife one time after they were married and having a lot of fun. I can't recall doing much with them in particular, but I enjoyed my time with the other kids that were there on the trip and playing with them at the hotel. This was a great experience for me and I would have loved to have more memorable moments like that. My father was a Mason and his wife was part of the Eastern Star, so as an adult, I remember going to a couple of their big events that the organization had sometimes. My father became a whole new person around his friends than he was with me alone. He seemed more outgoing, fun, talkative and affectionate. He seemed like he was proud of me, proud to be my father, and happy to have me around him and his friends. Times like these reassured me that he did love me; he just doesn't know how to express it well. I am grateful that my father was in my life. We sometimes expect things out of people that are not in them to give to us. As children, we see our parents as being perfect, but we have to realize that they are learning, growing, and they make mistakes. This is a part of acceptance and forgiveness.

So after my father got remarried, my dream had changed to thinking maybe my mother will meet someone else too and get remarried. I would bring it up, but my mother would not even entertain the thought. She clearly had no interest in getting remarried for the third time. There was only one man that I recall that I believe my mother may have had any type of interest. He was a bishop of a church and he lived in California. I have no idea how they even met since he lived miles away. My mother was saved, sanctified, Holy Ghost filled and fire baptized. So I know their connection was spiritual and God focused. I know he would write her, send her pictures, and they would talk on the phone occasionally. We even moved to California for a short time when I was very young and we lived with a woman there. We attended church there and I remember witnessing demons being cast out of people for the first time. I was use to a lot since we were Pentecostal and attended a Church of God in Christ (COGIC) type church, but I had never seen anything like this. I remember this experience being wild and scary, but we were told to keep your hands on the Bible during the deliverance and you would be protected. I am so thankful for those types of experiences with my mother.

I still did not see my mother date him or any other man while we were there. I am not sure how long we lived there before we returned home and I never knew why. My mother was very private so she didn't discuss her "business" much unless she was in the sharing mood. The Bishop and my mother appeared to be close friends. One day she told me he was interested in marrying her when I kept inquiring and asking questions about him. I encouraged her to marry him because I wanted to see her with someone. Besides, he seemed like a good guy from what I knew, which wasn't much, but she still did not entertain the idea of getting remarried. Whenever I would bring the subject up, she would say, "What do I need a husband for? Or she would say, "I ain't trying to take care of no man." So that dream of her being married again and having a male figure in the house was crushed too.

Representation vs. Relationship

I believe growing up in a single-parent home created distance in my relationship with my father. I didn't get to spend as much time with him as I wanted. Since I did not spend much time with him, I did not know most of my family on my father's side. My father bought me many things that I asked for, but I did not feel like we communicated much when we were together. I didn't feel like I really knew my father like I wanted to and should know him. I didn't feel like I knew his innermost thoughts or feelings. I didn't feel like he really knew me either. I often longed to have long conversations, a lot of laughs, and great experiences together. I remember I use to call him on my birthday, so he could wish me a happy birthday. Now that sounds crazy even saying it. After years of doing that, I decided to stop calling him on my special day. I didn't understand why he couldn't take the extra step to just call me and wish me a happy birthday like I did when it was his. I sometimes wondered if he remembered that it was even my birthday. My father was into taking pictures and doing creative things with them. He also created a calendar every year that included some pictures he had taken and important dates with the most important being my birthday. So if he looked at that calendar regularly, then he knew. I guess he got used to me calling.

I remember spending time with him when someone passed away on his side of the family. That is when I would see and hang out with his side of the family. I was excited to be around my family, but at the same time, it felt so awkward because I did not know them. After the funeral, I would not see them again until someone else passed away again. Looking back on this now, I wonder if things would have been much different if my parents never divorced or if it would have still been like this because that was just how my father was. I believe it was just his DNA, his personality. He was an independent but a laid back type of man. I wonder if he even spent much time with his family when I wasn't around and what were the family dynamics like. I wonder what life was like when he was growing up and what type of relationship he had with his mother, father, siblings and family. I wonder if he was trying to protect me from something. I wish I knew this information and more, but I really didn't know my father like some people would know their parents.

My father was in my life and a part of my life, but I just didn't have a deep relationship with him. As a result, I didn't know a lot about my paternal grandparents or that side of my family. I remember my paternal grandfather passed away and I said to myself, "I am going to make a personal effort to spend more time with my grandmother and get to know her." Little did I know, that opportunity would never come because she ended up passing away some days later and we were right back at another funeral the following week for my grandmother's funeral. The crazy part of that was that my grandmother and grandfather had been divorced for several years but she passed away right after he did. I always thought she must have still had a deep love for him even though they were apart. Now that is some real, serious love.

I don't remember my father attending many of my activities that I was involved in growing up, i.e., little league cheerleading, band concerts, marching band, even prom. He did not help me with my homework or attend school conferences. I do not even remember praying together. I did attend church with him whenever I was over his house, but his church was very different from what I was used to. At my church I was used to people dancing/shouting, loudness, falling out, the choir blowing, Sunday school, Pre-Service, real service for TV, and a very long day. At my dad's church, it was a lot quieter, no dancing, no running, singing from the hymn books, and only one service. We were in and out and back home in no time. I do however remember him being there for some of the very special moments in my life like the Ms. Ohio Teen pageant I was involved in, my graduation, walking me down the aisle at my wedding, and he came to the hospital after I gave birth to my first born child, my son. Having a child is such an exciting time in your life, and I was so happy to see my father by my side. I had a C-section though and they had me so drugged up that I could not even stay awake while he was there. I tried so hard to snap out of it and stay awake to enjoy the moment, but nothing worked. I kept dosing off and apologizing and after a while he was gone. At least he came to the hospital, though, so for that, I am forever grateful. I kept my son involved in many activities, but he did not attend those either. Wouldn't it be nice to wave a magic wand and make your life and parents the way you want them to be? We all know that is not realistic but it sounds good to say anyway.

I loved my father dearly, but I always wondered why he didn't call or come around more. Why didn't we spend more time together doing fun things? Why would he let someone keep him away from me? Why didn't he support me or encourage me more? Why didn't he come get my son and do Grandpa/grandson type stuff? Why didn't he tell me he loved me more? Even though I figured he did love me...I mean he is my father, but why didn't I hear it? I would have loved to go to a father/daughter dance together, to the park, fishing, camping, Disney, shopping, movies etc.... Well, I never got to experience these things with my father. Through it all, I can truly say my father was a wonderful man. He was active in church and he attended regularly. He loved and believed in God. He served in the military. He was a hardworking man and always kept a job. Even after he retired from the post office, he still worked at a pharmaceutical company.

My father was independent, very intelligent, and business savvy. He loved taking pictures, playing cards, using computers, and eating candy. I do not hold a grudge against him nor was I ever bitter toward him for not coming around or calling more often. Did I get mad at him, oh yes! I didn't stay mad long though and I didn't get stuck there. Could my father have done more and been there more frequently? Yes! I believe he could have. I also believe there were some challenges based on factors that prohibited us from having a closer relationship such as his personality, his upbringing and family dynamics, his lack of knowledge regarding being a father, life experiences, and his communication skills. Sometimes I would distance myself and stop calling or going around because he never put forth the same effort as I did. Now I regret doing that because that is time that I can never get back and I am learning that I can't always expect other people to do what I would do. Sometimes we expect to pull things out of people that are not in them. So when they cannot meet our expectations, we are disappointed.

How many of you had both of your parents in the household, but they really weren't there or you really didn't get to spend much time with them? How many of you did not have either parent living with you in your household at all? How many of you do not know one or both of your parents? Sometimes we think our life is bad or wish it could be better, but someone else is experiencing something significantly worse than we are. We have to learn to see the positive in every situation we are in and thank God for our blessings whether big or small. Many times we take the negative route and look at what we do not have or how we wish it could have been better or different, or what we could have had or even had more of. If we put on our positive glasses every day and looked at the glass as half full instead of half empty, I believe the world would be a happier place to live in and we would value life and everything in it a whole lot more.

My life experiences have taught me to view life differently, but it is not always easy, and I have to remind myself when my thinking gets off track or when I need to refocus. My truth is that my father did not live in my home with me, but I did have my father in my life and for that, I am thankful. Maybe if my parents had not divorced I would have had a closer relationship with my father, and maybe not. When my parents were still married, my father was a great father to my older siblings. To this day, they talk very highly of him and considered him their own father. My father was a provider for his family. Whenever I was in a bind and I had exhausted all my other options, if I called my father and asked for help, he was there to help. That is my daddy!

All a part of the process: Learning to love me

Growing up, I was very quiet. I was not considered popular in school and I was not really trying to be. I had several different friends that I use to hang out with at different times and occasions. I did not like talking in front of the class or in large groups. I would talk one on one or when I got to know you. I was an average student. I did my homework most of the time, had decent grades and hardly ever got in trouble. I wasn't motivated to excel in school though. It was just a routine thing that I did to get through it and graduate. I did my homework and studied independently. My mother attended my school conferences and I was sure to hear her mouth if I wasn't on top of things. If I got a C, I would get an earful to do better. If I got anything less than a C, I was sure to be on punishment. I hated when I had to get something signed by my mother that was not to her standards and return back to the teacher. If my parents were more involved and more hands on, I believe I would have been more motivated to work harder and would have done much better in school. Looking back I see the importance of studying hard and striving to get excellent grades. One thing I knew for sure, quitting was not an option.

I am more hands-on with my children than my parents were with me. I tried to learn from my life experiences — what was present or lacking in my childhood, what my parents did well or not so well — and incorporate those things into parenting. Being a parent is not easy. It is so much to learn and so much on your shoulders, especially for MOTHERS. I have not been the perfect Mother to my children. I don't believe any parent is perfect. I know there were some things that I could have changed or could have done better but I must proclaim that I am a great mother. I love my children dearly with all my heart and I want the best for them. I have tried to protect them, teach them, bring them up in church, and teach them about God and how to pray, and inform them about life/people. I am a good role model for them. I instill good values in them and support them. I have also informed them to respect themselves and others especially their elders. I will always motivate and encourage them and push them to be the very best they can be. I will continue to learn from my mistakes so that I can become a better ME to be a better mother and person for them.

Growing up I struggled with low self-esteem. I am not sure what age that started but I know it existed. If I had to guess, I would say in junior high school is when it really became noticeable. Being dark-skinned back in the day was not cool and was not considered pretty. You had to be light-skinned with really long straight or curly hair and a small build to be considered in the beautiful category. So here I am a dark-skinned girl growing up in a light-skinned world. I was not skinny but an average-sized girl, with big eyes, shoulder-length course hair and a gap in the middle of my teeth. I even rocked the wet Jheri curl style at one time in my life when it was popular. I was comfortable with my size and height but I always wanted to be lighter — even a couple shades lighter would do. Sometimes I would hear people crack jokes or make comments about dark-skinned people and called us names like blacky, purple, tar baby, midnight, etc. The best phrase you frequently hear people say about others that did not make the cut is, "She is pretty to be dark-skinned or big." Why does it have to be a stipulation on what someone perceives or defines as beauty? Can't they just be pretty because they are?

People picked on me because of the color of my skin and my big eyes. Kids can be so cruel to each other, but it was nothing compared to how kids are these days! The bullying is out of control. It was apparent that if you were light-skinned, you were more popular and you got all the attention from the boys. As a dark-skinned girl, the boys either put you in the "friends" category or "booty call only" category. When I did get attention from a boy, I was geeked. Thank goodness I didn't get so caught up on craving attention that I accepted whatever they dished out in order for them to accept me. The guys who accepted me for who I was and what I looked like were the ones who got my time and attention. The ones who had a side-eye agenda might have got a smile or two, but I wasn't falling for the banana in the tailpipe trick. I didn't need attention that bad. So because of how people treated me, based on my outer appearance, that affected my self-esteem and I am sure contributed to me being very shy and quiet. It is a natural feeling to want to feel accepted.

It is sad, but some people are so shallow that they never accept you or make an effort to get to know you because of how you look or who you are. When I looked at magazines or watched videos, I saw small, light-skinned girls/women and they were the most beautiful women you ever saw. Where are the beautiful, confident women that look like me? In Genesis chapter 29 it describes the story of Laban, who had two daughters, Leah and Rachel. Jacob came and stayed with them. The Bible states, "There was no brightness to Leah's eyes, but Rachel had a beautiful shape and was lovely to look at." (Genesis 29:17) Jacob fell in love with Rachel and offered to work for seven years for Laban in exchange to have Rachel's hand in marriage. Leah was the oldest and it was not proper to give your youngest daughter away in marriage before the firstborn. I used to feel like Leah, the one who was overlooked for someone else. I felt like one who was looked at as not as appealing and beautiful to others. The one that was a good friend but never pretty enough to be the pick. I desired to be a Rachel until I learned to love me for me.

I remember wanting to be lighter so bad after high school, that I started using skin bleaching cream on my face. It appeared to lighten my face but it made my skin discolored and not even toned. I remember going to visit one of my childhood friends that I grew up with in Dayton, Ohio, and I was trying to find where she lived. I was lost and was asking around to find her place. When I finally found her, she told me some guy told her that a light-skinned girl was looking for her. Of course, she didn't expect to see me. I remember feeling overjoyed inside that someone considered me light-skinned. I didn't know that cream had worked that well. Maybe he was half blind, but I accepted it anyway. Using that cream got old and I didn't like the way it made my skin look discolored, so I eventually stopped using it to lighten my skin complexion and accepted my natural color. It also amazed me that the race I identified with was harder and less accepting of my dark skin and beauty than other races. Also, younger people were less accepting than older people. I would get so many compliments from older people and other races. It was their seeds that were planted that I am sure made me look twice at myself to want to see what they saw in me. This world would be a better place if everyone made an extra effort to encourage and build up each other up with acceptance and positivity.

As I became an adult, I realized that light-skinned women faced similar issues and insecurities as dark-skinned women. It appeared that the lighter your skin was, the better you were treated and the more opportunities you had. Being light-skinned did not exclude you from being picked on or not liked. Someone once told me that they were the lightest one in their family and they did not like being different and they were teased or picked on for being light. Some people want to be darker and even tan their skin to get darker. One of my brown-skinned friends that I went to school with experienced similar complexes regarding her skin color, low self-esteem and insecurity issues as well. I never in a million years would have guessed she struggled with having self-esteem issues. She seemed so confident, so popular, so well liked by everybody, including the boys. She felt insecure because she fell in the middle of the light-skinned/dark-skinned chart, and she did not like her skin color or feel accepted either. She shared her feelings of having low self-esteem, not feeling beautiful and not getting a lot of attention from boys.

I have realized that many women of all shades of color felt disliked, insecure, or were unhappy with their skin complexion or looks for one reason or another. Most people also believe that back in the slavery days, the light-skinned women were in the house and dark-skinned women were in the field. After reading up on this, I found that it was the opposite. The wives of the masters did not want the light-skinned pretty slaves parading around their husbands, so they were working the fields and the dark-skinned, less attractive women were working in the house. To this day you still have people who are stuck on color and what is considered beautiful, but people, in general, are more accepting of all shades of color now.

The fact is that you have to accept the skin you are in and understand that beauty starts within. When you are confident, it shows. When you are confident, you stand out in a crowd and people can tell that you are secure in yourself. If people think you are not confident, some people will try to use that to their advantage to mess with you or bring down your self-esteem. Do not try to be like someone else, find the beauty in you. Rock your own style and enhance your best features or qualities. Find what works well for you, your body type, skin tone, etc....and rock it to the fullest. I once heard supermodel Tyra Banks say that you should be able to take a brown paper bag and make it look good. I took that statement and ran with it. I remind myself of that concept often and I refer to it when talking to others.

Women, when you are confident, you should be able to find a way to rock anything and look fabulous. When I am feeling beautiful, I walk different, I talk different and I feel good. When you walk with confidence it will just ooze out of your pores. You will feel it and others will see it and know that you are one confident woman. When I am having a bad hair day or maybe I am not that excited about my outfit choice for that day, and I let insecurities creep in, that shows too. If you are having a bad hair day, rock it like it just got done or disguise it with a nice hat or scarf. Even when your self-esteem increases, those insecure moments will try to rear its evil head. This is where positive affirmations will shut this right down. Do not look for others to validate or pour into you. Encourage yourself! Tell yourself how beautiful you are and how great you look. Learn how to turn those insecure thoughts into something positive that will work for you.

It is so important to tell your children how beautiful/handsome they are at a young age to build their self-esteem so when society places their value or image of beautiful on them, they are not moved by it. Encourage them to love themselves how God created them to be. Teach them to speak life into themselves and be a good example for them. Show them what being confident looks like. They are always watching you. Always remember God created us in his own image and his creation was good. Inform them that people may talk negatively about them but encourage them to ignore what other people say and believe what is true. Inform them that sometimes when people talk about you, it could be because they are jealous or they are battling insecurities themselves. People that do not have your best interest at heart will do or say things to hurt you or to tear you down.

I built my children up instead of tearing them down. My son was always confident and secure about his appearance. In fact, I would have to remind him to stay humble and not get too cocky or conceited. I tell my daughter all the time how beautiful she is. She knows she is beautiful too. If there is a mirror in the room, no matter where we are, she will make her way to it and smile, sing, dance, model, you name it. You have to pry her away from the mirror. I remind them of how intelligent they are and that they are leaders and not followers. Tell your children that it is okay to be unique and different. That is what makes them special. Teach them to set their standards high and do not lower it for anyone to try to fit in or be cool. Discover the real you, what you like and dislike. Discover your own style and own it. It is okay to stand out in the crowd in a positive way. Also inform them to stand up for what they believe in, even if they have to stand alone. Teach them to "always be YOU and love yourself unconditionally." It is important to know that your inner beauty, your personality and the way you treat others is significant. If your outer appearance is beautiful but your personality is horrible and you treat people awful, you do not appear so beautiful. I believe everyone no matter how beautiful they are has something they may not like about themselves or wish they could change if they could. Some people grow to love the very thing that they at one time hated about themselves. We cannot focus on things that we cannot change. We have to focus on our positive features, enhance them, and work with it.

Now I am a confident woman of God. I have accepted my dark skin and my big eyes. If people have something to say about it or do not like me or the way I look, oh well, that is their issue, not mine. When I was rejected by men or overlooked, I finally saw it as their loss. It does not feel good to be rejected, but it does not feel good to be mistreated either. I had to work hard on loving and accepting myself. Once I did, my self-esteem increased and I began to believe what people had always told me, that I am beautiful. I knew that I was a good person and I began to recognize my worth. If there was something about me that I was not happy with and I could change, I worked on improving it. For example, as an adult, I got braces to close the spaces in between my teeth. Not many adults were wearing braces at my age at that time. I became known as the lady with the braces. At first, I thought about what other people would say about me being grown at my age with braces. I also thought to myself, why didn't my parents get braces for me when I was younger? Then I told myself who cares what other people say or think. Do what you want to do. Do what will make you happy and do it for you and only you. So I did just that. I knew that I would be satisfied with the outcome at the end so I went for a consultation and I got my braces. I rocked my braces and I owned it. It was one of the best things that I ever did! I didn't have to hide my smile anymore or feel insecure when I opened my mouth. Now many adults get braces or other things done to fix their teeth or enhance their smile. Some people have spaces in their teeth and don't change it because it represents who they are. It is their signature. They are confident and they rock it well. Do what works for you!

As we age and have children most women gain more and more weight over time. I know I fit into this category. I have tried since college to lose weight. I have tried almost every diet plan available to man. I have tried to alter my eating habits, exercise, personal trainers, weight loss pills, etc....I was usually able to lose some weight but I could never hit my ideal weight. It seemed like when I would lose and get to a certain weight, I would plateau and then start back gaining. I get so discouraged at times and want to give up, and many times I have given up for a period of time and then started back gaining weight. I use to get so depressed about my size and how difficult it was for me to lose just one pound. At times I did not want to go anywhere for others to see me; I didn't feel comfortable in my clothes or confident about myself. I have had two cesarean sections, which have made it even harder to tighten and lose this stomach. The weight loss struggle is really real.

Obesity runs on both sides of my family. I have a family history of diabetes, heart disease, chronic renal failure, high blood pressure, high cholesterol, congestive heart failure, arthritis, cancer, respiratory problems, among other things. I am still not where I would like to be, but it is these generational curses of infirmities that keep me fighting to lose weight and achieve my goals. No matter how much I lose and regain, or get discouraged, I will not give up on me. I am healthier now than I have been in years. I have never been a runner, but I have linked up with my Sole Sisters Black Girls Run! and now I can run. I am a runner and I keep working hard to improve my endurance and pace. I attend Boot Camp Cincinnati where I flip car tires and do more than I have ever imagined myself doing. In order to maintain or lose weight, I make a conscious effort to eat healthier and exercise. I walk confidently in the skin I am in, while I work on where I want to be. I have not conquered this battle yet, but I will.

A great example of a person with confidence is Donald Trump. People talk about him all the time and badly. They call him a racist. They talk about his toupee. They attack his character. The crazier he talks, the more people support him. He is confident in what he says whether right or wrong. People talking about him or disliking him has not stopped him from pursuing his dreams and goals. Because Donald is a confident man, he has persevered. Even if you are not a big fan or supporter of Mr. Trump, there is a lesson or two to learn from him. Be comfortable in your own skin and walk in it with your head held high no matter what!

Since my parents divorced at a young age, it shaped my belief that I would never go that route and I vowed that when I got married, I would never get divorced. I told myself that I did not want my children to feel or experience what I did growing up. I also grew up living with my mother and sister who both were not married. My mother had gotten two divorces and my sister had never been married. The thought of this made me become very anxious. I began wondering if anyone would ever want to marry me. I had been in a few serious relationships in my life. One relationship was a great relationship with my best friend. We had so many wonderful times together. One day he decided he wanted to see other people. This was a low blow to me. We had a great a relationship, but why was I not good enough for him? So I informed him that if we saw other people, we would break it off completely. He was not going to have his cake and eat it too. In order to protect my heart, I knew I had to separate myself completely from him. That day I lost my best friend and that was the hardest part of it all.

This decision hurt me to my inner core, but it was a decision that needed to be made. Everything reminded me of him and I would just bust out in tears at any given moment thinking of him and what we shared. For years I questioned myself on whether I made the right decision and even regretted my decision at times. My self-esteem took another hit. I wondered was I not light enough, pretty enough, sexy enough? What was it? What was it that he was looking for? What did I not have, that he wanted? Well, what I realized was that we were still young and had a lot of growing, living, and learning to do. I was also grateful that he respected me and our relationship enough to feel comfortable enough to share how he was feeling, even if I didn't agree or want to accept it. I also figured out that I could not continue trying to figure out why he had made the decision he made. I realized that it wasn't about him and what he wanted and needed. What about my wants and needs? I am a wonderful person and a good woman. His loss is someone else's gain. Everything happens for a reason and what we had was for a season and that season was over. I had to pick up the pieces, dust myself off and find a way to move on. I loved myself more than I realized and I deserve the best. I deserved to be loved unconditionally.

So as I regrouped from that relationship, I continued to pursue my college education. I continued to meet other guys and casually date, but nothing serious. Since my mother and sister were not married, fear began to creep in my mind and the enemy led me to believe that I may not ever get married and that no one would commit to me. I questioned whether I would be single forever or if I would be good enough for anyone. I had my life already planned out, but this was not how I had it planned. I did not want to be single forever. I wondered what was in store for my future and I started feeling pressure to get married. It seemed like in my mind, everyone had a man but me. This was so far from the truth but when the enemy starts messing with you and putting crazy thoughts in your head, you have to rebuke those thoughts or you will begin to believe them.

As a young adult, I started hanging tough with my close friends. You cannot do this now, but back in the day we would drive around the town to different neighborhoods and waste gas looking to see who we would run into and meet. We met a lot of guys that way too. I started going to the clubs occasionally, then I ended up finding myself going several nights a week. Some nights I would even go alone. I had a ball dancing, seeing people I knew, laughing, talking, and meeting new people.

One night I went out with my friends to this newer club downtown and I had fun as usual. As we were leaving the club late on this dark nice night, this guy was standing on the outside of the club and started talking to me. So we talked and I giggled for a short time and he asked for my telephone number. I gave him my number and we began talking and spending a lot of time together. We hit it off really good. At the beginning, we were inseparable. We started going to clubs together, hanging out with other couples, and he treated me well. I was still in a vulnerable state from my previous relationship and I was tired of being alone. I thought he was cute and sexy and on the bad boy side that you are attracted to when you are young. So he won me over. We ended up moving in together, which is something I had never planned to do. After living together that is when things got real. We had a lot of good and fun times but we had some rocky times, too. That is expected in relationships, but I noticed that I was beginning to change as person. I remember feeling disrespected by him and I was ready to end our relationship. You see, when you are not married it is easier to end things and walk away than when you are married, especially when you do not have any kids. I have always been the type of female that would walk away in a heartbeat. I have been in a place of loneliness before but never desperation. Some women feel like they always have to have a man to validate them, but that was never me. I loved him but I was ready to call it quits. He was different and wounded with a lot of past hurt and pain. He could be the nicest person one minute and then the most difficult person in the world the next. This relationship was unique and quite different from any relationship I had ever been in. He apologized and pleaded for us to stay together and work things out. I was hesitant because part of me had empathy for him regarding what he had experienced during his childhood. I knew he was a good guy at heart. The other part of me was ready to walk away from this relationship and never look back. I chose to give our relationship another chance.

As time progressed he had proposed to me and we got engaged. This is what every girl dreams of, plans and fantasizes about. This was my dream come true! My fear of not getting married and no one wanting me was going to be destroyed. So off to planning this big wedding I went. As I was planning, I would sometimes have doubts about whether I should get married or not, but I did not have enough guts to call it off and inform everyone that this was not going to happen. I also often thought about the money my parents had already spent toward this wedding. How could I break the news to everyone? How could I disappoint everyone? Then those old thoughts started creeping back up in my mind again. I worried more about what other people would say and how other people would feel more than I did about my own feelings and well-being. I kept telling myself, "Things will change once we actually get married." We will be married; he will change. We will be husband and wife. We will be committed to each other and we will be happy…. Right? Isn't that how marriage works? Wrong! Well, that is not how it worked for me anyway.

So we got married, but it wasn't happily ever after. The wedding was nice and we all looked great and we had a great time, even though there was a little drama at the reception from his side of the family. We continued to have some good times, but we also continued to have some very bad times — and more of the bad times than the good ones. During this marriage, I experienced a lot of financial hardships, disrespect, a lot of heartbreak, pain, and disappointments. Things didn't change when we got married, things actually got worse. I endured a lot of verbal and emotional abuse and as a result, I would get so angry that I was physically abusive toward him. I didn't know how to accept the way I was being disrespected, disregarded and treated or how else to react. I didn't know how to channel my pain or anger toward him. The police made a few house calls to our residence and one time an officer told me that I could not continue to live in this matter. It will not end well if you do, he said. There was even one incidence where we were arguing and our neighbor called the police and said that I threatened to kill him. Now even though he made me so mad that I would want to hurt him, we both agreed that I never threatened to kill him. The police ended up coming, handcuffing me and taking me to jail. I never imagined going through anything close to this in my life. I am so thankful for God's favor, especially in the midst of a storm. I was released after a very short time and when I went to court the case was dismissed.

My husband was a hard worker but he played hard, too. We didn't do much hanging out together anymore; he was hanging out without me. I found myself home alone a lot. I was in my last year of college and I became pregnant. We were both excited but I was nervous. I begin to think, maybe this will be the very thing that changes things for us. Maybe this will slow him down. Well, it didn't. I spent my first Mother's Day alone as well as several nights and other significant times. While he was out running the streets, I was at home doing the parenting.

The arguing continued and just became worse and more frequent. We would throw verbal blows back and forth and curse each other out like it wasn't anything. We both said things that hit below the belt to hurt each other. If he came at me and my family, I came back at him and his family. It became a battle to see who could win at hurting the other person the most. It was one emotional roller coaster. We separated at one time and we ended up getting back together to try to work things out. Things would get better momentarily and then things would get outlandish again. I was truly miserable. I didn't want my child growing up in this type of environment, but I was reminded of the promise that I made to myself that I would never divorce. Do I stay and continue to try to work on this marriage and keep my family together or do I walk away to find my true happiness? I signed us up for a marriage conference at our church and he never showed up. I wanted to attend counseling and he would say he was willing to attend, but he would never follow through. He showed no interest in being a husband, a father, or being a willing participant in this thing called marriage. It takes the efforts of two people to make a marriage work. I spent many days and nights alone crying and praying. I realized that I had made a huge mistake by marrying this man who truly didn't take our vows seriously. He had no respect for our marriage. I was tired and had had enough.

Well despite many efforts, things did not improve. I was not the perfect wife, but I gave this marriage all that I had inside of me to give. I knew our marriage was over and I decided to leave him. There were a couple of factors that I considered that helped me to decide it was time to leave. One was in this relationship I was not my normal self. I was not me! I lost myself, who I was, how I was raised and who I was developing to be. I finally realized when you find yourself doing things that are out of your normal character and that are not in a positive light, it is time for a change. The second factor was that I was afraid that if we did not go our separate ways, someone was going to get hurt, killed or end up in jail. This marriage was extremely unhealthy and although I didn't want to break up my family, a child still has to endure the effects of their environment. Children can also detect when something is wrong, no matter how much you try to hide it. So because I didn't have enough courage to call the wedding off, I got married and was still faced with a difficult decision of going through a divorce. For my sanity and the best interest of my child, I left one day when he went on one of his weekend excursions with his friends and never looked back.

I planned it all in no time. I went to my mother's house because we were arguing and I could not get any peace. If I tried to talk on the phone, he would be disrespectful in the background and he even disconnected the phone. I gathered my child and I left. It was the Kentucky Derby weekend so I knew he was planning to leave. I knew him so well that I knew the pattern and was aware of what he was planning to do before he did it. So when he wanted to go hang out in the streets, he would start an argument to create an opportunity for his escape. So I knew he had planned to go with his friends to the Derby and when he did things like this, he never would even call home to check on his family to make sure we were okay. He was married but living the single lifestyle with his single friends. So I spent the night at my mother's house. The following day, I called and arranged for movers to come out and I called and obtained a storage unit for our things. I went back home and packed up our things and the movers came the next day and moved it into my storage. I had packed and moved out in two days while he was out of town partying. When he decided to come home, he came to an empty place because his family as he knew it was gone.

This was the start of the next chapter of my life. We were separated for a while before I finally decided to file for a divorce. When I left, although it was frightening to start over, I felt like a ton of bricks had fallen off my shoulders. I was sad. I felt like a failure but I also felt a sense of relief. Divorce is similar to death. You get used to being with someone for so long that you grieve their absence from your life when they are no longer there. It takes time, but eventually you have to let go of the past and work on your healing.

I had never experienced physical or verbal abuse before in any of my relationships until this time. The funny thing is, I knew it was abuse but I never viewed it as real domestic violence. I remember thinking that I would rather for him to hit me than to say the dreadful things he used to say to me and endure the mind games that he used to play with me. I thought words cut deeper and hurt longer than any physical contact could. I didn't view myself as a domestic violence victim or perpetrator until several years later. This is a hard realization to admit. I was able to muster up enough courage and strength to remove myself from this situation and relationship, and I can proudly say that I have never been in a violent or abusive relationship with anyone else since.

My life after the divorce was still a very difficult time. Although we were not together anymore, we still had to see and interact with each other because we had a child together. He also had a close relationship with my family, my mother in particular, so I had to still endure seeing him at her house, sporting events, at holidays, etc. ... I believe he thought, "If we are not going to be together, I am going to make her life a living hell here on earth." The verbal abuse and disrespect continued and actually became worse as if it was not bad enough. I never imagined I would still have to stomach this after I left him. Sometimes we would see each other and would walk right pass each other like we were strangers. Other times there were often moments of some sort of public display of reckless behavior. I was in and out of court on several occasions for years.

Working together on any level as it related to our child was nearly impossible. Every week there was a different issue and something different to argue about. Our visitation schedule from the court was a joke, and even with my paperwork in hand that stated that my son was supposed to be with me, when he did not follow the schedule the police could not and would not do anything to help me. I was often told to take this to domestic relations court. When I took it to court, nothing happened there either. He was such a con artist that when we would go to court, he would make up all types of lies and have them convinced that he was the world's greatest dad and I was the angry ex-wife. I had no voice, no advocate, and no help from the court system. The system had truly failed me. At one appearance, I was told, "It is better to have a not-so-good role model for your son than none at all." I was floored! I thought to myself, "That is not good enough for my son!" How dare someone tell me that? I bet she didn't follow that same principle when it came to her children, but apparently, that was good enough for mine. She was blessed that I have never been a violent person (before this relationship) and that God was on my side and hers because I could have surely treated her to a big upper cut to the jaw for saying something so ridiculous to me like that. I failed to take this battle to God and let him direct me and let him fight for me — so instead God let me handle it. While I kept my hands in it, I lost the fight.

One time when I dropped my son off at Kmart for his visitation, I went into the Kmart to pick up a few things and I came right back out. I came out to find the side mirror to my Infiniti QX4 hanging by a wire. I was livid. My ex-husband and his girlfriend swore up and down they didn't do it, but that was awfully coincidental I thought. I tried to get the video from the store, but I was unsuccessful with that too. So I had to come out of my pockets to get my mirror fixed, and the perpetrator(s) got away with it. Nothing was working out in my favor. I had to wonder, where was the love, God? Why do I keep getting the short end of the stick? Who is on my side? Why can't anyone see the truth? Why is he getting away with all of these lies and wrongdoing? I was furious. I was angry and I was bitter. I didn't realize at the time that I was falling right in the trap of the enemy to deeply hate and hold on to all these negative feelings. I was walking in unforgiveness daily. I was on a path of destruction. "To whom ye forgive any thing, I forgive also: for if I forgave any thing, to whom I forgave it, for your sakes forgave I it in the person of Christ; lest Satan should get an advantage of us; for we are not ignorant of his devices." (2 Corinthians 2:10-11)

My self-esteem was tested yet again and actually took a major beating during this process of marriage and divorce. Remember, this was already a demon I struggled with most of my life. The enemy knows how to use your weaknesses to lure you down the wrong path or cause you to make some bad decisions. Things you have struggled with in the past have a way of coming back up to haunt you. I was told that I was fat, ugly and that no one would ever want me. I was often called things other than my actual name. Some days I have to admit that I did feel like these words, and other days I would have to convince myself that I was beautiful and worthy to be loved and be happy.

I had to work on finding myself and my relationship with God. When I tried to meet men and get back into the dating game again, it was a difficult task for me. I wasn't ready for a relationship, I just wanted companionship. I decided I didn't feel like staying on the roller coaster of relationships to find out this person was really like this or like that. I needed to take time for me and work on me. So I stopped dating for several years and even prayed to God to keep the temptations away.

I spent many days confused, angry, and trying to figure out my next move. I hated myself for not calling off the wedding. I hated myself for stopping to even talk that night at the nightclub. I couldn't believe this was happening. I didn't want to get too serious with anyone else that I met at the club. I wished so many times that I could rewind my life and change my story. I hated my ex-husband. I had so much rage, anger, unforgiveness, and resentment built up in me toward him. I could not stand to look at him, see him, to be in the same room with him or talk to him. My guards were up and the walls were standing strong and tall. My idea of marriage was tainted. My actual marriage made me resent marriage and I vowed to never get married again. I remember telling my friends, "If I ever tell you that I am getting married again, take me to the hospital to have me checked out!"

I spent a lot of energy on fighting for what was right, fighting for peace, and fighting for what I thought was best for my son. One day I was waiting for my son to return from his extended visitation with his father for two weeks. I got a call from a lady from the courts stating she had received a call from my ex-husband regarding violation in the visitation schedule. He said that he didn't get to keep our son for a long enough time frame (even though he sent me a letter specifying what dates he would pick him up, keep him, and bring him back home) and he wanted to keep him longer. She asked me would I be willing to allow him to keep my son some additional days. I politely told her, "No, I would not," and shortly after that we ended that call. At that point, I had reached my breaking point and I said to God, I don't know how strong you think I am, but I am so tired of this. I can't take this anymore. I am not doing another thing. I was so frustrated, I wept and cried out to God and I remained still and did nothing. In the past I would have called my ex-husband, argued, got in my car and trotted myself to where he was to go get my son, and/or called the police. We had been to court on numerous occasions without much being done. I even kept a journal of dates that he didn't pick him up as scheduled, if he was late picking him up, if he didn't bring him back as scheduled, you name it. He proclaimed to the courts that I made it all up and I was an angry ex-wife that wanted him back. That was the new label that was placed on my back and told to everyone. Remember none of these actions had helped me in the past, so this time I did nothing. After I cried out to God, I got a phone call from my ex-husband that he was bringing my son home. God will fix it, if you let him! This was the start of a new day for me because there was a shift in the atmosphere. Our relationship began to shift in the right direction. Do not get me wrong, our relationship was not perfect, but I begin to learn how to fight in a different way. I was starting to become wiser and smarter with my fight. I began to argue and talk less, and pray and trust God more. This was not always an easy task and I did not pass the test all the time, but when I did let go and let God fight my battles, they became a lot easier.

Shortly after college, I had the desire to move out of town. I prayed about this on many occasions seeking direction about moving. I decided Charlotte, North Carolina, was my next step in life. I started doing research on the city, schools, cost of living, weather, etc.... I planned my first visit of many with my son and my sister and we all fell in love with the area. I could definitely see myself there and we had a ball. Even my sister, who I thought would find every reason to talk me out of moving, said she wouldn't mind living there too. I went to a women's conference in Atlanta and I heard Joyce Meyers preach and she said sometimes God is waiting for us to take a step. She said sometimes having faith means "go" and then God will show you; not show me first and then I will go. So I thought, "Okay, let me try this out since I am unsure of what to do. I am going to take a big step of faith and plan to move." I was ready for a new beginning, to meet new people, go to new places, and restart my life. I also thought this would eliminate the current drama and stress in my life. I began looking into places to stay and started applying for jobs.

Everything seemed to be falling into place, but I still had to face one big hurdle. I had to either get my ex-husband to approve of the move or go back to court again. Of course since coming to an agreement had never been our solution before, I thought this time would surely be no different. When I discussed the idea with him to get him to agree to us relocating, he informed me that he would fight me until the end and he did. So off to court we went. After a few appearances, my petition to move was denied, with no chance to reapply for a year, and family counseling was recommended. Once again my plans had failed and my heart was shattered into a million pieces. I asked God, "Why didn't you just tell me no, instead of having me go through all of this misery? If He did try to communicate it to me, I missed the memo. I was furious, to say the least. This man still had control over my life! I thought I would have to fight over the visitation schedule and never imagined I would be told that I could not move. I had full custody of my son and I was very capable of finding a job, taking care of him and starting a new life. I was sad and very disappointed for a little while, but I had to suck it up. I strongly believe everything happens for a reason, so I knew there was a reason that I needed to stay put. There is someone that needs me or something that I still need to do. As disappointed as I was, I had to force myself to be content in my current situation.

It wasn't until years later that I realized why my plan to move was not the best plan for my life. My sister became critically ill and after several tests and biopsies, she was diagnosed with liver cancer. My sister had always been sickly but nothing to this degree. It started when we were out of town at a T.D. Jakes women's conference. I believe this was the first year for the Megafest event. She was so weak and tired and she kept sitting down to rest. I picked up on it and asked her if she was not feeling well, and she confirmed my notions. Needless to say, for the first time we were not able to enjoy the conference, which is something we looked forward to attending every year. So we went back to the hotel so she could rest. Little did I know that what lay ahead of me would change the course of my life forever. Shortly after we got back home, I noticed my sister's eyes were now yellow/jaundiced. I knew this was an indication that something was going on with her liver. I didn't want to alarm her, but I told her that she really needed to make an appointment to visit the doctor. I still had expected this to be an easy fix and everything would be back to normal.

We initially received a report that it was not cancer and we all were ecstatic, but they were not sure what was going on. Then she was misdiagnosed with some disease I had not heard of before and had to research on to quickly find out that was not the correct diagnosis. When we finally got the report of the "C" word, things got really real. I felt like I couldn't talk to anyone about it. I didn't even want to say the word cancer. I didn't want to speak anything into existence, so I was very careful with my words if I did talk about it. We went through a series of tests, surgeries, chemotherapy and doctor visits. It is very hard to see and take care of a loved one that is very ill. I am a nurse by profession, but that went out the window when it came to my sister, my best friend. This couldn't be happening. It seemed like she would get better and I would have hope. Then she would go through chemo and it would just wipe her out and my hope too. She lost weight very fast, something she always wanted to do but not like this. It was too difficult to discuss what we were going through so I didn't talk about it to others until it got to the point that I had to share it. She would even try to hide things like how she was feelings or complications she was having from me and my mother. She just tried to endure the pain and complications without complaining or telling us. We could usually tell though when something was wrong. She didn't want the sympathy and she was always a private person to begin with.

The crazy but not so crazy part about this is that God showed me that it was going to happen years before it happened. I had several dreams about it and I saw my mother and I at her funeral. When I would have this dream, I wrote it down in my journal. I pleaded with God not to take my sister and I had hoped it was just a bad nightmare that would never come true. I asked God what these dreams meant. These dreams started in May 2002 and I couldn't tell anyone about them. I didn't want to even entertain the idea of it coming to past, so I kept it to myself for years and just prayed about it. In July of the same year, I had a similar dream regarding my sister. I believe my sister became sick in 2005 and it was this year she received her diagnosis of cancer, three years after my dreams started. My sister fought a good fight to the end. The doctor ended up removing about 80 to 90 percent of her liver. They said they would shave off a little more then test it, and it was still tested positive for cancer. So they would shave off a little more then test it again. They removed as much as they could possibly remove, and her liver was still testing positive for cancer. They said they would explore more treatment options for her, but her life expectancy was not long. I believe they gave her one good year to live.

Toward the end of this journey, she told me she was tired of getting cut on. She was back in the hospital again and I could tell she was getting tired and losing hope. The doctors started talking about life insurance policies and hospice. I was so angry at them. They seemed so insensitive to what was going on. I needed them to give her reassurance of hope and to keep fighting. I remember her asking me if her eyes were turning yellow again and I told her yes. I tried to be so strong for her, but I was literally dying on the inside. This was one of the most difficult things that I have ever in my life had to experience. I thought going through an unhealthy marriage, divorce, and aftermath was bad — that was nothing compared to this. She was so strong during this entire process. This was the strongest that I had ever seen her throughout life. I had a strange feeling that when we took her to the hospital that last time, we would not have here very long, but I still pushed that thought out of my brain. I kept telling myself that this is not happening. I remember walking out of her room and just sobbing. I remember one day the nurse expressing her concern because my sister would not eat or talk to anyone, which was out of character. She said the only thing she had said was that she wanted them to do everything they could possibly do for her. When I came to visit that day, I was able to get her to eat and talk to me. She knew exactly who I was and I called our mother so that she could talk to her. We never got to bring my sister back home again, and on October 16, 2007, she transitioned to eternity and passed away. Ironically on this very same day in the year 2015, I am writing this portion of the book about my best friend.

After she passed, I didn't know how I would make it another day without her in my life. I cried all the time. My heart was aching so bad that it felt like it was oozing blood from being stabbed and shot several times. I asked God how could I go on living? I asked why He took my sister away from me? What am I supposed to do now? Maybe I should have prayed for her a little more. Maybe I should have prayed differently. I wished I would have stayed at her side 24/7, but I had so many other responsibilities of being a single parent and working. I took for granted that she would get better and be released home. I was mad at God! I became depressed very quickly. I did not want to work, eat, sleep, or do anything I normally enjoyed. I isolated myself from everyone. I stopped going to church on a regular basis. I still loved God, but I felt like everything in my life was a struggle. I didn't understand why life had to be so difficult. I began to reflect on all the areas of my life that I had struggled with. I struggled in nursing school and had to work harder than everyone else to succeed. I struggled with low self-esteem the majority of my life. I struggled with my finances off and on for many years. I struggled with bad relationships, a failed marriage, lost friendships, broken promises, and betrayal. I struggled with my faith, hearing clearly from God and becoming closer to him. I struggled with failed business endeavors. I struggled with witnessing division and corruption in my church. I struggled when I saw couples that seemed so right for each other and so in love, get divorced. I struggled with losing weight. I struggled with my many battles in the courtroom. I struggled with not being able to move out of town. I struggled with haters being jealous and trying to attack me and bring me down. I struggled with my inner insecurities. I struggled with getting along with my ex-husband. I struggled with being happy. You name it and I probably struggled with it in some form or fashion. After I returned to work after my sister passed, I had to struggle at work too. Now this too? What is next God?

I questioned if I was that bad of a person. I wondered and was scared of knowing what the next steps of my life were. I could not seem to get a break anywhere. The adversary has a way of really using people and things to get to you when you are down and broken. He knew I was in a vulnerable state, and it was his mission to try to destroy me. I had to push myself to do everything I did. I did not want to leave my house and most days my bed. I felt myself falling into a deeper and deeper hole that I knew if I didn't start climbing out of, I would be swallowed up and buried deep in it. Positive self-talk became my new best friend. I told myself, if I didn't work, I would lose everything that I have worked so hard for and my son and I could be homeless. I told myself to fight through this pain. I forced myself to do things that I really didn't want to do. Instead of turning toward God for support through this, I turned away from him. I felt so empty and disconnected without him, too. I knew he was right there with me and waiting for me with open arms, but I was too mad at him to ask him to help me through this. Truth was, I didn't understand why it happened. I didn't understand why this had to be my sister's story. I began to try to fill my void with partying, hanging out at the clubs again, meeting men and entertaining unhealthy relationships. My behavior was reckless and I made a lot of mistakes along the way. I kept trying to fill this open wound and void in my heart, but nothing corrected the problem.

My sister lived with my mother practically all her life, so this was a major adjustment for her as well. She would call me all times of night wanting to go to the hospital for everything. One time she called and told me she could not breathe. I rushed over there to check her vitals and she was fine. I told her that she was breathing fine and she told me she knows how she feels. I believe she started having panic attacks because she was now living by herself. How can I grieve when I have to worry about my mother and stop whatever I am doing to run check on her? I was so stressed and depressed it is a miracle I am still here and sane enough to write about it today. The years following my sister's death, I had to fight with everything in me to keep living. I had a son to live and fight for. Even when I was extremely mad at God, he never stopped loving me and he never gave up on me. I was able to crawl out of that big, deep, dark hole that was trying to suck me in and slowly I began living again.

Years later, looking back on my journal, as I was planning to relocate and praying about confirmation of that, God was showing me that my sister was going to pass away. I was so focused on me and what I wanted that I missed the message. In reality, though I didn't understand, God was trying to communicate with me through my dreams and I was in denial because I did not want to lose my sister or anyone else for that matter. My sister even told me about a dream she had where a couple came to her and asked her to move to North Carolina and take care of their child. The man was very familiar to her. She told him she didn't know because she didn't want to leave her mother. She began to ask him questions: "What about my job? What about insurance? What about my mother?" The man replied, "Don't worry about that. I have everything taken care of for you. I will build you a new house from the ground up and fill it with furniture. It will be big enough for your mother to come too." She described it as a huge mansion big enough for the whole family to live in, but still have their own privacy and space. "I will pay you more than you are making now. I will take care of you," he said. When I looked this dream up in the dream book, I discovered that man could mean Jesus or helper, husband means authority/God, wife means covenant, baby means new beginnings, new house means new life or change, moving. I wrote this dream down in my journal too like I did my own and we talked about it, trying to figure it out.

One day God brought that dream back to my remembrance. God was telling her that he had a new place he was preparing just for her. He didn't want her to worry about anything because he had it all covered. He had a plan. He didn't want any of us to worry about where he was taking her. What a mighty God we serve! John 14:2-4 says, "My Father's house has many rooms; if that were not so, would I have told you that I am going to prepare a place for you? And if I go and prepare a place for you, I will come back and take you to be with me that you also may be where I am. You know the way to the place where I am going." God was trying to prepare me for what was to come, but because I didn't understand and was looking at things through my natural eyes instead of through my spiritual eyes, I made this journey much harder for myself than I believe it should have been. My life began to spiral downward and out of control, but thanks to God, I was able to get myself back on track.

Over the next several years I experienced several great losses in my life. After that experience, I found myself in a similar situation again with my father. He became gravely ill and I had to witness him get worse, lose weight, and eventually pass away. He went from being admitted into the hospital for something minor as diarrhea to being discharged home with severe heart failure and hospice. So in 2009, I had to help plan and attend my father's funeral. This was another blow to my heart. I saw my father as so independent and so strong. So to see him wither away before my eyes was devastating. I never imagined seeing him not being able to care for himself, to drive, to be able to do something simple like walk or eat. One time I was visiting with him and tears began to flow from his big beautiful brown eyes down his face. I had never in my life seen my father cry or be too emotional before. I had to contain myself and my emotions as my eyes welled up with tears. I had to be strong for him as he always was for me. Since he was married, I had no control or could not make any decisions for him. I felt left out of the decision- making, planning of his services and was hurt from this entire ordeal, but God kept me through it all. I was there until the end and his funeral was very nice. Even though our relationship was not all that I would have loved for it to be, I am very proud to call him my daddy.

Since 2007, I have had a series of deaths of people very close to me. I lost my best friend, who had been sick since graduating from high school. I could talk to him about anything and he knew and loved God dearly. He was funny, he was a great communicator, he was encouraging and he was a true friend. He was helping me get through the loss of my sister and then he was gone, too. He passed in the same month but the following year after my sister died. I felt like I was walking around in a bad dream that I could not wake up from. On the day of his funeral, I drove around and around trying to find the church to say my goodbye until we would meet up again. But I rode in circles and was unsuccessful. My GPS was very unreliable that day. For the life of me, I never could find that church. That tore me a part. I wanted to tell him to tell my sister hello for me and give her a big hug and kiss. It must not have been meant for me to be there. I am not sure if I could have even handled it, but I wanted to be there for him like I always had been before. Then I lost my first cousin who had diabetes, and one of my aunts who had several health problems. I was still fighting the enemy in the midst of this storm.

Shortly after that, the pastor of my church who had battled breast cancer for many, many years passed away. I really felt lost without any spiritual covering from her. She was simply an amazing woman and the best pastor, mentor and teacher. She could preach and prophesy her short self off! She was so in tune with her members and what they were going through and she would call you out of the blue to check on you and speak what thus said the Lord. She was a mighty and anointed woman of God. She even gave of herself so freely even when she was going through her own battle. When my sister was in the hospital, she was right there. She wanted to know what was going on with her members. I remember when I didn't tell her my sister was sick and she found out through someone else. She immediately called me and told me she was going to whip me with a wet spaghetti noodle because I didn't tell her. I was never one to run to my pastor and tell them all about my storms. I would tell a few close people to me and deal with it until it cleared and the next one came. She was one of a kind and she truly loved and wanted to be involved with her members and their lives. Not just a select few of her members but all of them, including little old me. She spoke over my life several times and I had never had a pastor do that before. Some of the things she prophesized over my life years ago, have either already manifested or is starting to manifest now. Her passing was very difficult and I couldn't believe it because she was so powerful and it seemed like there was still so much work left yet for her to do. I began to question God again. I thought, "Now God, I know you needed her to do a lot more of your work. She was really on fire for you and she sacrificed a lot for your people and the kingdom." What is really going on? We need her here. The world needs her. Her family needs her here. I need her here! Why, why, why take her? Why now? Why didn't you heal her again? What are we supposed to do now? When things happen to us, we do not always understand why, but we have to trust the plans of God. "Trust in the Lord with all thine heart; and lean not unto thine own understanding. In all thy ways acknowledge him, and he shall direct thy paths. Be not wise in thine own eyes: fear the Lord, and depart from evil." (Proverbs 3:5-7)

Your life can change in an instance

If all of this wasn't enough to endure, my firstborn son, who has always been healthy and athletic, became ill. I picked him up from football practice after a long, busy and typical fall day and everything was business as usual. We picked up something to eat and arrived home to complete our day. My son was feeling good and he had no complaints as he retreated to his room to do homework. We then went to bed, ending the night like our typical day. When we woke up the next morning our lives were completely changed forever! As we ran around the house and packed to leave for a weekend road trip, my son remained in his room all morning. After I had gotten everything pretty much together, I went to his room to see if he was ready to go. When I saw him, I almost fell out. His face was swollen up significantly and looked disfigured. Every time I think of that moment, it reminds me of the episode of Martin when he was in the boxing match with Thomas Hearns. At the end of that match that he lost badly, the way his face looked all distorted was similar to how my son looked. I could not understand what was happening.

My first thought was that it was an allergic reaction, so I drilled him with a million questions. I asked if he had eaten something new? I asked if he had taken some medicine overnight? What had he done differently? His answer was no, no, nothing. I checked his body for any evidence of a spider bite, but I could not find anything. I proceeded to call the pediatrician, and they asked the same questions. Thankfully they were able to get him in to be evaluated. He was seen by a different pediatrician in the same office and she was baffled as to what could have caused this swelling. She came to the conclusion that it must be an allergic reaction to something, but the cause was unknown. We were given some prescriptions to fill to combat this reaction and rid this swelling.

While we were at the pharmacy waiting for the prescriptions to be filled, the pediatricians' office called us back. The doctor requested that we come back to the office so they can check his blood pressure and urine. So back to the doctor's office, we go as we wait for the results. My son had just had a physical about a month prior to this for football and his blood pressure and everything was within normal limits. So I didn't imagine anything major to be wrong with him. To my surprise, the doctor reports that his blood pressure was high, he had blood and protein in his urine, and he had a significant amount of weight gain since his physical. She wanted us to report directly to Children's Hospital for further evaluation and she was going to inform them that we were on our way. What a day this has been thus far! A day filled with unexplained surprises and many detours. I never expected to wake up that bright sunny, beautiful morning with a checklist of planned activities to complete and end up in the emergency room with many unanswered questions and a mystery illness out of the blue. By the time we arrived at the emergency department, the swelling in his face had decreased, but swelling was noted now in his legs and ankle. After further examination, they wanted to review his lab work and we would be released to follow up the following week. Well as soon as we got our hopes up to leave, we were informed that his lab work was a little concerning and they wanted to admit him into the hospital for further evaluation.

Our new journey consisted of a series of tests, a series of questions, a kidney biopsy, and a diagnosis of lupus nephritis, hypertension, and acute kidney injury. I was not aware of anyone in my family that had lupus. His father was not aware of it in their family history either. I later found out that one of my aunts on my father's side of the family had lupus, but she had passed away. This is why it is so important to know your family and the family history. Lupus is an autoimmune disorder that can affect many different systems/organs since the body turns on itself and attacks its own tissues. This can cause inflammation and tissue damage and can attack any part of the body. Those individuals with lupus can suffer from oral ulcers, arthritis, pain in their joints, skin rashes, heart problems, kidney problems, brain abnormalities, seizures, photosensitivity and abnormalities in their blood. This disease can cause you to be very fatigued. Anyone can be affected by lupus but women and those of African, Asian and Native American decent are more likely to be affected by this disorder. In the general population 1 in 1,000 people can be affected by lupus.

When I received that initial report with a diagnosis from the doctor, I was in shock. This cannot be true or real. No, not my son! Maybe I am dreaming and I need to hurry up and wake up from this nightmare. My life seemed so surreal. This was very real. Eventually, we were discharged from the hospital with several medications and follow-up blood work.

The swelling started gradually increasing again and he woke up one fall morning with his eyes almost completely swollen shut. I had to break the news to him that we had to go back to be admitted to the hospital. His body kept retaining fluid causing him to swell up. In a period of time of about two weeks my son had gained about sixty plus pounds. As I looked at my son, it was someone different looking back at me. This did not even look like the son that I had raised for fourteen years. There were several days of daily weight checks and intravenous medications to try to rid his body of this excess fluid. They would eliminate some fluid and more would return. They were having a difficult time getting this issue under control, and if the fluid accumulated too much it would start affecting his heart and lungs. In additional to this, his kidneys began shutting down. He had difficulties using the bathroom. Something that had always been so normal for him was now very difficult. He was in a lot of pain all over his body from his skin stretching from the fluid and weight gain.

He was very weak and his gait was unstable. I remember encouraging him to go for a walk because I didn't want him to get pneumonia from immobility. We walked downstairs to the cafeteria and he was so weak that I had to grab a wheelchair and push him around and back up to his room. His coordination was off balance and he would stumble just walking to the bathroom. His spirits were down because everything was happening so fast and he could not understand what was going on in his body and why. He would look at me with that look in his eyes that said, "Mom, fix this! Help me!" But I couldn't. As a child, you are so used to your parents, particularly your mother, being able to fix things and make things better. This was one situation that I had no control over in the natural realm. I as his mother could not fix this! I felt as if my back was pushed up against a tall brick wall and God was saying, "Will you trust me? Will you trust me even with your only son?" This was one of the hardest times in my life. It is very difficult as a parent to see and care for your child who is sick. At this point, I had a decision to make. I could either let this situation beat me down or I could trust God and fight. I chose to trust God and fight. I had to be strong for my son. I began to pray like I had never prayed before. I began to speak life over my son. I began to trust God more. There were moments that I would have to leave his room and break down and then I would regroup and go back in the room with more strength and a smile.

The doctors could not get the fluid under control and there was a concern that the fluid would begin affecting his organs. So he had to have an urgent surgery to have a temporary catheter placed so they could begin dialysis to pull off this fluid. When they took him to dialysis, they took the equivalence of four 2 liter bottles of fluids off. He looked dramatically different. He was starting to look more like my son. As they continued to remove the fluids, the less he weighed and the more he looked like himself. They said he would have to undergo dialysis for a little while, but my son had a praying mother and grandmother. After about a month, the dialysis was discontinued.

He had to start receiving an aggressive chemotherapy medication. This medicine required a lot of fluids, an overnight stay in the hospital to be administered, and several severe side effects. The doctors said normally patients have to receive this medication once a month for several months. My son received two treatments. He went from taking no medication to taking about seven or eight different medications. Now he is taking only two. His kidneys went from barely functioning to fully functioning. The best part about this life-changing experience is that my son touched so many lives during this experience. There were two doctors on his treatment team that continued to follow his progress and check on him. They not only took good care of him physically, but they encouraged him, supported him, inspired him and really showed us compassion. One of these doctors helped him with his schoolwork and he was so touched and inspired by our story that he decided to specialize in that area to become a nephrologist.

God also placed so many people in our life that willingly helped us through this journey. Because we were in and out of the hospital for several months, my son missed a significant amount of school. I remember when we were headed back into the hospital for the second time; his counselor called and told me that she recommended that I withdraw him for the remainder of the year and enroll him into a virtual school. She also informed me that the school would gladly let him return the next school year. He was attending the No. 1 school in Ohio and a top nationally ranked school, so it is very fast pace. If you miss one day, it is like missing at least a week or more of work. His counselor was concerned that he would miss too much work, making it difficult for him to catch up, therefore placing him in jeopardy of failing the ninth grade. My son was already feeling blue with the overwhelming events occurring in his life, so I cried at the thought of even telling him — as if there was not enough bad news and now this. When I broke the news to him, he was definitely opposed to it and I was not fond of the idea either. I was afraid if we took that socialization out of his life, he could possibly hit a very low point like I had done in the past.

One of his football coaches frequently checked on us to see how things were going. He would pick up his homework from school and bring it to the hospital for him to complete. One of my friends called someone from her church to come and have communion with us at my request (since our pastor had passed away) and stayed for a while and helped him with his schoolwork. Someone that I had recently started to get to know was a teacher and she came to our house and tutored him for free several times after he was discharged.

When I tell you the favor of God was upon us...the favor of God was upon us! Not only did he remain enrolled in his current school, but he was able to get caught up on his work and return back to school after his Christmas break. He did not fail his freshman year, he returned to football his sophomore year, added track to his already busy schedule his junior year, became one of the captains of the varsity football team his senior year, and he recently graduated from this very high school. My GOD is awesome! God never left us nor forsook us even during these trying times. Words cannot express how appreciative I am for everyone who encouraged and supported us during this season. Many of his friends, the football team, my friends and family came to visit us and helped to cheer us up.

When my son got sick, I started to blame myself. His father and I had gone through so many years of conflict and pain. My mother would always say about my son, "Something is going to happen to him because y'all keep arguing over him." So when he actually got sick, those words kept ringing loudly in my ear. Did we cause our son to get sick because we could never get along? Did my mother cause this because she kept speaking those words over his life? Even though I was feeling guilty about him getting sick, I did not have time to dwell on it because he needed me to be strong and take care of him. God even sent someone to me that had no idea what my mother had always said or how I was feeling, and she confirmed that my son being sick was not my fault. The ironic thing about all of this is that God changed the relationship between his father and me. I told him that we needed to get along for the sake of our son and for once in his life he finally agreed. Normally if I said the sky was blue, he would insist that it was green. God helped me move past the many years of hurt, pain, unforgiveness and bitterness and let it go. His father apologized for his past behaviors and actions and stated he was ready to move forward while working together to care for our son. It was then that our relationship did a 360 degree turn and we were able to communicate and be civil with each other. We are able to communicate with each other, pray for each other and support each other for our son's sake. Now that does not mean that we are BFF's and the enemy does still slip in to try to cause division or take you back to the way things used to be. But guess what? The devil is a liar! I refuse to go backward and relive my past. God makes all things new.

Here is a brief excerpt of how my son was feeling during this difficult ordeal: "It's my first year of high school and it's going pretty good. I have good grades and football is coming along great. It's Friday morning and I'm going out of town. The sun is almost out and it's a pretty humid morning. As I'm going through my morning routine something feels different. I feel heavier. I feel more sluggish than usual. I feel as if I'm not myself. So I look in the mirror and see that my face is swollen up. I was afraid. I didn't know what in the world was going on with me and my body. When my mother sees me, the shock in her face still appears in the back of my mind to this day. She calls my doctor instantly and tells her the problem and that we are coming in. As the day goes on, the swelling decreases.

"When we arrive at the doctor's office, she checks me and asks me a few questions about what happened. Initially, she brushes it off as an allergic reaction and she gives me a prescription for antibiotics and a few other things. So my mother and I go on with our day and go to get the antibiotics from the pharmacy. I wait in the car patiently while she gets them. When she comes back she has this strange look on her face. She tells me the doctor called her and we have to go back to the office so she can check something else out. We go back and the doctor says my blood pressure is high and they found blood and protein in my urine. I'm sent immediately to the emergency room. I go back to the room and get examined and blood was drawn for testing. The doctors there tell me he will let me go on a condition that I come back in for a check-up on Monday. He leaves the room to get my paperwork, then gets stopped by a nurse and eventually comes back in and closes the door. The plan has changed again and I have to be admitted into the hospital immediately for further testing. With the snap of a finger, my life has changed in a day.

"I'm lying on a bed in an unfamiliar room that's holding me from the outside world. My mother and father are there and a few of my friends. The room is medium sized and has a television with cable. I can smell the different scents and odors from other patients being housed in this room before me. A bathroom connects to the room with a shower inside. There are fancy paintings on the walls of cheerful things, but I feel as if I'm a prisoner in a box. I'm hooked up to an IV and have a hospital gown on. I am young and confused, I feel miserable and irritable. As the day progresses, I realize I will be here for a while. The doctors and nurses come in and out hourly and I hear no news. Then when I finally get the news, it is not what I expected. They gave me a diagnosis."

A Mother's Love

A year after my son became ill, my mother became very ill. She ended up in the hospital with kidney failure. She had an urgent surgery to have a catheter placed so that they could begin hemodialysis. Does this sound familiar? I was dealing with a similar situation with my son one year prior. God was preparing me for what was coming to help me be strong. My mother was really sick. Her doctor had been trying to convince her to start dialysis, but she had refused until a couple months before she became sick. The plan was for her to get surgery to have a catheter placed in her abdomen to start peritoneal dialysis, but before she could get the surgery she was hospitalized. She never told us how serious her health was, but it soon was revealed. One of my mother's siblings died on the dialysis machine. One of her other siblings was on dialysis for several years as well until she passed away. This may be one of the reasons why she was so adamant about not doing it. She prolonged it for as long as she could until she was forced to begin dialysis.

One day I went to visit her at the hospital and she was confused and very short of breath. She had just come back from dialysis and she looked like a train wreck. Something was definitely not right! I informed the nurse, who initially blew me off and didn't think anything significant was going on. I insisted that something was wrong. She called someone in to take my mother's vitals and check her oxygen level and they were unable to obtain it. The next thing I know, the room is filled with hospital staff members. They ended up placing her on oxygen, drawing blood, new medicine was ordered and eventually she was transferred to the intensive care unit. She spent several days in the ICU before transferring back to the initial unit she was on. She was eventually well enough to be discharged and she came to stay with me because she was still very weak and needed a lot of assistance. I had to arrange for an ambulance to pick her up three times a week to take her to hemodialysis because she was unable to walk and I wasn't able to lift her to get her there. I had to arrange for physical therapy, occupational therapy, and a nurse to come out to visit her. She slowly began to get stronger, her blood pressure improved, she started gaining weight and she was improving. At this time I learned that the doctor had given her one year to live if she didn't go on dialysis, so she waited for another year. She said, "God didn't bring me this far to leave me." I overheard her tell the home nurse that she was ready to go and that when she was still here after a year, she decided to go ahead and proceed with the dialysis.

My mother was improving and she had a regular

routine. And despite the leg cramps she was feeling better after starting dialysis. She thought maybe she should continue with the hemodialysis instead of switching to peritoneal dialysis. I wasn't sure that was the best option because they had already placed the catheter in her abdomen to start the peritoneal dialysis when it healed and the temporary catheter that they were using for her hemodialysis would have to be removed. If she continued with hemodialysis she would have to have another surgery to remove both catheters and place a permanent catheter or fistula in, and I thought that would be too much.

Now I sometimes wonder if maybe we should have gone that route. When we switched to the peritoneal dialysis, she began to go downhill again. We had so much trouble with her catheter and her dialysis machine. Then her appetite decreased significantly. My mother loved food. When she refused to eat and take her medicine, I knew something was really wrong. She ended up being hospitalized again. She refused practically most of the care and procedures they were suggesting so they didn't know what else to do for her. Her doctor suggested hospice. I was so opposed. My life over the last few years felt like a living nightmare. Could all this really be happening to me? My mother kept telling me that she was tired, but I refused to believe that I would have to live on this earth without her. I kept trying to encourage my mother to keep fighting. In my heart and spirit, I knew what was ahead for me but I refused to accept it. I began to pray to God to give me strength to endure this upcoming journey. My mother was my everything, my world, and my backbone. I called her practically every day before all of this. She has always been there for me. I couldn't imagine my life without her. I knew what dark place that I went to when my sister died and I refused to let myself go back to that place.

In less than a year after my mother became ill, she passed away. My life has been forever changed again. It seems like that timeframe is so fogging. I pressed through the pain and continued to pour into myself to make it through. I surrounded myself with family and I stayed busy. I learned a lot from my mother, her life, and even through her passing. She was a blessing to so many people. When I felt weak, God strengthened me and made me stronger. When I felt like being down, God lifted me up and gave me unspeakable joy. Grieving the loss of someone so close to you is devastating. It creates an empty void that only God can fill and heal. Some people say that time heals and relieves your pain. Time does not erase your loss or pain, but it makes it more tolerable. You eventually learn to pick up the pieces and continue on with life as it is. I learned that when someone goes through losing someone, some people, be it family or friends, do not know what to say or do to help or support you. Some people ignore that it has happened and never bring it up. Some people say things like, "Well, they are in a better place" or "No more sickness, no more pain." Some people send cards, flowers, or food to show their love or support and others are nowhere to be found.

I saw a message of T.D. Jakes one day and he was talking about when he lost his mother and the grieving process. He said the pain was so deep when grieving that cards, flowers, sweet potato pie, etc. … could not help that pain. When he turned it over to God, that is when grief started coming up out of his spirit. This statement hit home for me and is so true. Grief is difficult, but you have to trust God and rest in him to move forward past the pain. Having a great support system helps this process. Do not be afraid to bring up the loved one that someone lost. It brings me joy when people discuss my mother, what she meant to them, how she touched them, or share a story about her with me. I appreciated when someone called to check on me to see how I was doing, especially during the difficult times of holidays, birthdays, Mother's Day. Be intentional about being supportive when someone is grieving and let them know that you are truly there for them during that time. God even used me to support, encourage and minister to others that were grieving while I was still healing myself.

I thought I was so independent and I didn't realize how dependent on my mother I really was until she was gone. I was dependent on her prayers and her faith to help carry me through. Now I had my own prayer life and relationship with God, but I realized that I felt more secure because I knew my mother was always in the background lifting us up in prayer. I started becoming more anxious about life. This became evident to me when I went out of town shortly after my mother passed away. I became so anxious about getting on that plane. All I kept thinking about is, my mother is not here to pray for my safety. I was both grieving and anxious all rolled up like one big ball of mess. My stomach was in knots and I became so sick that we had to pull over on the side of the highway and I had a vomiting episode. I proceeded to pray like I usually do when I fly, but you best believe that I was praying much harder this time.

My prayer life has changed significantly. I realized that I had to be a better prayer warrior for myself and my family. I realized that I trusted God but I sometimes placed limitations on Him. I serve a limitless God who is my protector, my provider, my guide, and my EVERYTHING! He hears and answers my prayers too. God reminded me to trust Him! "Do not be anxious about anything, but in every situation, by prayer and petition, with thanksgiving, present your request to God." (Philippians 4:6 NIV) God reminds me often that he is my comforter. God reminds me that I am the apple of his eye. God reminds me that nothing is impossible with him. He also reminds me to rest in Him. Casting all of our cares at God's feet and completely resting in Him is not always easy, but it is one of the best things we could incorporate in our lives.

I am so glad that through all of our failures, mistakes, and unfortunate circumstances, God still loves us, forgives us, and encourages us to walk in our purpose toward our destiny. He then uses our stories to bless and encourage others in their journey. After getting divorced, I decided to go back to school to pursue a higher education. I worked full time while attending college and I obtained my master's degree in Community Health Nursing. I chose a great career path that has afforded me a variety of experiences in my profession. I was able to build my first home as a single parent. I have raised an intelligent respectful son who has a bright future ahead of him.

I am now remarried with two beautiful biological children and a beautiful stepdaughter. I am working on living life on purpose, pampering myself more, and living a healthier lifestyle. My son's health is excellent. His recent appointment to the doctor revealed that his lab work was normal, his kidneys are functioning at 100%, and he has enough energy to play college football and run track while in his first year of college. I am still believing God for total restoration and complete healing for him.

Through a vision God gave me several years ago, a wonderful women's ministry has been birthed called Live2Move Women of Destiny, which consist of some powerful women of God. God has placed some wonderful people in my midst and he continues to bless me all the time. My relationship with God is stronger and deeper than it has ever been before and it continues to soar to new heights. Against ALL odds, I have persevered and I am still persevering! Guess what? You can too!

"Remember those earlier days after you had received the light, when you endured in a great conflict full of suffering. Sometimes you were publicly exposed to insult and persecution; at other times you stood side by side with those who were so treated. You suffered along with those in prison and joyfully accepted the confiscation of your property because you knew that you yourselves had better and lasting possessions. So do not throw away your confidence; it will be richly rewarded." (Hebrews 10: 32-35 NIV)

Pearls of Wisdom:

- It is a natural feeling to want to feel accepted, but learn how to love and accept who God created you to be. If others do not accept you, that is their issue.
- Build your children up early and speak positive affirmations over them often.
- Your pain does not have to be the end of the story.
- As children, we want our parents to be perfect and do everything right, but we have to realize that we all make mistakes. They may be doing the best that they know how to do.
- We have to be a witness to others. As we partner with God, we can bring others to Him.
- Stop letting the disappointments of your past dictate your future.
- Learn from your failures and do not let your failures define who you are.
- Failure is not final.
- In spite of your flaws, you still have favor

I OWN IT! SESSION:

1) Read Matthew 18:35. How does it apply in this story?

2) Look up John 16:33 and refer back to this scripture when you need encouragement to persevere.

3) Do you believe that the conflict between the parents contributed to their son's illness? Why or why not? Did his grandmother contribute to his illness?

4) In what ways do you feel you can help someone who has experienced loss and is grieving?

5) How can you help build someone's confidence/self-esteem?

6) What level of persevering do you believe she is in?

Conclusion

After reading this book I hope each story has inspired you in some way. As you see, we all go through different circumstances in life. Life happens to us all. Remember, you are not alone in whatever you have faced or experienced now or in the past. Let your past be just that — your past. Our past is meant to teach us, mature us, to help us become wiser and groom us to be better individuals as a whole. Do not beat yourself up because of your past and shortcomings. Every single one of us has fallen short in one area or another and has made some poor decisions or mistakes. No one is perfect but God. That is why God sent his Son to die on the cross for us and our sins. The blood of Jesus covers us from our past and cleans our slate. Ask God to forgive you of your sins and then forgive yourself, which is one task that can be very difficult to do. The adversary will try to keep you stuck in condemnation by continuously reminding you of your mistakes and your past. You can be set free from this bondage.

Let every experience good or bad be a lesson to learn from and a stepping-stone toward your true purpose. Take time to heal and then move forward into your destiny. Do not let the enemy keep you stuck when life happens to you. You can overcome anything. Even that! Do not let other people keep you bound either. People love to associate you with things that you have done in your past. They are quick to remind you of things that you use to do or how you use to be. Be just as quick to remind them that your past does not define who you are, nor does it define your future. Inform them that you have left those things behind you and you have been created new in Christ. "Therefore if any man be in Christ, he is a new creature: old things are passed away; behold, all things are become new." (2 Corinthians 5:17 KJV) "Remember ye not the former things, neither consider the things of old. Behold, I will do a new thing; now it shall spring forth; shall ye not know it? I will even make a way in the wilderness, and rivers in the desert." (Isaiah 43:18-19 KJV) God can make a bad situation better. God can make an imperfect person great. Remember, a failure is not final.

Forgiveness is vital to your healing. Forgive those who have hurt, abused, or taken advantage of you. Let it go! Nothing is worth missing out on the blessings and promises God has for you. Forgiving someone doesn't mean that the situation did not exist. It means that you refuse to remain a victim of the situation and you are moving on to be victorious over it. Forgiveness means that you are set free from the chains that have been holding you hostage for so long. Walking in forgiveness is not an option, it is mandatory and necessary. Pray and ask God to help you forgive yourself and others and be healed completely from it. Also, ask others for forgiveness if necessary.

Retrain your mind to look for and think positively in every situation, good and bad. Always remember, nothing is impossible to get through with God. Speak life over yourself daily. You are stronger than you think. You are more than a conqueror. Never give up on your dreams. Never stop fighting for freedom. Never give in to the negative thoughts and tactics of the adversary. Never give up on YOU. Life will try to break you down completely while the adversary will try to steal from you, kill you, and destroy you — but God. One key factor to keep embedded in your mind and being is, Against All Odds, Persevere!
"I'm stronger because of my hard times, wiser because of my mistakes, and happier because of my sad experiences."

__Resource Page__

1) Women Helping Women: This organization supports and empowers women from all   backgrounds who have experienced things like sexual assault, domestic violence, dating violence, abuse, etc. —
http://www.womenhelpingwomen.org/

2) Domestic Violence Hotline: 1-800-799-7233 or 1-800-799-SAFE — www.thehotline.org

3) Women Helping Battered Women:
http://www.whbw.org/get-help-now/resources/

4) Active Parenting Program: Effective parenting program — www.activeparenting.com

5) Health Resources and Service Administration: Maternal/child health and depression during and after pregnancy — www.hhs.gov

6) National Suicide Prevention Lifeline: 1-800-273-8255

7) Suicide Prevention Resource Center: http://www.sprc.org/

8) Motherless Daughters Ministry, Inc: motherlessdaughtersministry.com

About the Author

Veronica McCall was born and raised in Ohio and is a devoted wife and mother of two beautiful children and one step-daughter. She worked full time while she continued to further her education to obtain a Bachelor's of Science in Nursing Degree and then a Master's of Science Degree in Community Health Nursing. She has worked in the nursing field for over 19 years which has bequeathed her personal and professional experience working with the community.

Veronica's relationship with God started at an early age as she attended Sunday school and church regularly. This set a solid foundation for the women she is today. She has many years of experience mentoring teenage girls, serving others, and ministering to women. She has served as a greeter and a member of the outreach team at her church as well as served with other organizations within the community. God gave her a vision many years ago showing her a glimpse of her purpose and in 2014 a women's ministry - Live2Move Women of Destiny Ministries was birthed. She has a deep passion for helping others, for ministry, and Godly connections. Veronica is a powerful woman of God who is maturing in Christ as she walks in her destiny. One of her favorite scriptures that she lives by is Proverbs 3:5-6 KJV "Trust in the Lord with all your heart, and lean not unto thine own understanding. In all your ways acknowledge HIM, and HE shall direct thy paths."

www.ingramcontent.com/pod-product-compliance
Lightning Source LLC
LaVergne TN
LVHW011242080426
835509LV00005B/596